# K
# C

American Institute
of Architects
Guide to
Kansas City
Architecture
& Public Art

AMERICAN INSTITUTE OF ARCHITECTS/KANSAS CITY • HIGHWATER EDITIONS

*American Institute of Architects Guide to Kansas City Architecture & Public Art*
© 2000 American Institute of Architects/Kansas City

Cover: An eagle sculpted by Louis Saint-Gaudens guards the entrance of the New York Life Building (1890), Kansas City's first "skyscraper," home to the multinational energy company UtiliCorp United. *Photograph by Brad Finch.*

Back Cover: In 1994, a helicopter installed R.M. Fisher's *Sky Stations*, commissioned as part of Kansas City's One-Percent-for-Art Program. *Photograph courtesy of the Municipal Art Commission.*

This book was made possible through generous grants from the City of Kansas City, Missouri, the Kansas City Design Center, many of our design and construction partners, and others who also value our community's architecture and public art.

Printed by Richardson Printing, Inc. in the United States of America

Library of Congress Card Number: 00-103973

ISBN 1-888903-06-6

# Contents

# **S**upporters

THIS GUIDE WOULD NOT HAVE BEEN POSSIBLE WITHOUT GENEROUS CONTRIBUTIONS FROM THESE ORGANIZATIONS AND INDIVIDUALS:

### PRINCIPAL SUPPORTERS

The City of Kansas City, Missouri

William T. Kemper Foundation

AIA/Kansas City

The Hall Family Foundation

Hallmark Corporation Foundation

DST Realty, Inc.

Turner Construction Company

The Arts Council of Metropolitan Kansas City

Capital Electric Construction Company, Inc.

Johnson Controls, Inc.

The Builders' Association

### FRIENDS IN THE DESIGN AND CONSTRUCTION COMMUNITY

Ammon Painting Company

Mr. J. Philip Kirk Jr.

Mark One Electric Company, Inc.

Midwest Titan Incorporated

Associated General Contractors Inc./Kansas City Chapter

CNA Insurance Companies and Victor O. Schinnerer & Company

Overland Park Development Corporation

Linda Ervin Young Fund of the Kansas City Architectural Foundation

A. Zahner Company

A.L. Huber Construction, Inc.

Carthage Marble Corporation

DiCarlo Construction Company

JE Dunn Construction Company

KC Heritage Construction Co.

KONE Incorporated

Lockton Companies

Western Fireproofing Company of Kansas City, Inc.

Greater Kansas City, Missouri, Chapter 100 of the National Association of Women in Construction

Economic Development Corporation of Kansas City, Missouri
Shughart Thomson & Kilroy, P.C.
Construction Specifications Institute/Kansas City Chapter
Bratton Corporation
Ochsner, Hare & Hare
Otis Elevator
RNC Enterprises, Inc.


AIA/KANSAS CITY MEMBERS:
ASAI Architects
BNIM Architects
CDFM² Architecture
Devine Deflon Yaeger, Inc.
Gould Evans Goodman Associates
HNTB Corporation
Ellerbe Becket
Mr. Richard L. Farnan
Gastinger Walker Harden Architects, Inc.
HOK Sport, Event and Venue Architecture
TK Architects, Inc.
Wiedeman Architects Inc.
Bucher, Willis and Ratcliff Consulting Engineers and Architects
John Lawrence Daw and Associates Architects
Peckham Guyton Albers & Viets, Inc.
Peters and Associates
Piper-Wind Architects
Shaughnessy Fickel & Scott Architects
Shaw Hofstra + Associates
Susan Richards Johnson and Associates, Inc.
Warner-Nease-Bost Architects
Junk Architects, P.C.
Dean Graves Architect
Mr. Richard D. McDermott

# oreword

WITH THIS PUBLICATION WE CELEBRATE OUR METROPOLITAN AREA'S architecture and public art. The intent of the book is to provide residents and visitors with a catalog and tours that encourage appreciation and understanding of our special architectural heritage. This guide is the result of a thoughtful and cooperative effort to record the changes — including renovations and additions — to Kansas City's significant buildings and public art in the 20 years since the last guidebook was published.

Our fascination and delight with the built record of the area's history is not for its own sake, though that is reason enough to applaud the extraordinary character of this place. The designers, buildings and art we celebrate here are also important for the lessons they offer, the stories they symbolize, and the aspirations they embody. These buildings and sculptures are a representation of the tribulations and triumphs of the people who have created this community, individuals whose pride and sense of purpose were so palpable that they took on built form.

Our celebration reinforces a belief in the value of collaboration and a faith in the promise of innovation. Ideally, it inspires an optimism that will carry us into the future.

Only 150 years after the beginnings of the city at the confluence of the mighty Missouri and Kaw Rivers, we stand at the threshold of a new millennium. We are both exhilarated and apprehensive about the changes ahead, and we can learn much from those who faced overwhelming challenges before us. We inherit a surprising, rich, and multifaceted built environment with an extraordinary and unprecedented character that could not have developed anywhere else.

Our place, our Kansas City, calls us to continue the work. We hope the efforts documented in this book inspire others to strive to achieve a measure of the success we celebrate within these pages.

Richard Farnan, AIA
November 2000

# Architecture in Kansas City

IN 1979 THE KANSAS CITY CHAPTER OF THE AMERICAN INSTITUTE OF Architects (AIA/KC) published its first guidebook to the architecture of our city. In the two decades that have followed Kansas City has seen the addition of many outstanding buildings and the loss of several old ones. For this reason alone, a new guidebook for Kansas City architecture would be warranted. The year of this publication, however, brings two additional compelling reasons to overview the built assets of our city. The new millennium provides a time to both look to the future as well as review the past, and the year 2000 also marks the 150th anniversary of the founding of the City of Kansas City, Missouri.

To this end the Kansas City Chapter of The American Institute of Architects has joined together with the Design Center of Kansas City to publish this celebration of Kansas City architecture. The intent of this book is to give the reader a representative visual image of Metropolitan Kansas City through its exceptional buildings, urban design, and contemporary environmental public art. The material in this guide was drawn from many sources and all entries have been carefully deliberated by an editorial committee made up of distinguished architects, educators and historians.

The reader will find — arranged in 12 geographic districts — examples of the work of some of the area's finest architects and artists, as well as a number of entries by individuals of world renown. At the beginning of each geographic area is a guide map, along with an introduction to the overall significance of the area. All entries can also be found in the index, listed by architect/artist, as well as by project name.

These geographic areas were defined primarily to assist the user in efficient use of time to schedule and visit the subjects of this book. As it happens, the geographic divisions tend to parallel closely the patterns of growth and development in Kansas City and recognize the individual styles of Kansas City, Missouri; Independence, Missouri; Kansas City, Kansas; and Johnson County, Kansas.

The content of the new guidebook was based on the 1979 edition, with the recognition that the years since then have produced an abundance of outstanding examples of architecture, most of which speak to a maturing of the art and practice of the architectural profession in Kansas City. Additionally, Kansas City's One-Percent-for-Art Program, given new impetus in the 1980s, has provided a body of public art that enhances many of those examples of recent architecture. The private sector also has recognized the value of public art and many privately developed projects carry that commitment with them.

Because the size of the book necessarily had to be limited, the Guidebook Committee invited a jury of Kansas City architectural professionals to assist in evaluating new projects, as well as editing entries from the 1979 book. Kansas City architects were solicited to provide examples of their works since 1979 to be considered for inclusion in the new book. Scores of projects were offered for consideration and the jury selected more than 300 examples to be included.

The result is a guidebook that is not complete, but one the committee believes offers a comprehensive look at the history and development of the role of architecture in Kansas City's built environment. To keep the size of the book manageable, the committee excluded monuments, fountains and other free-standing structures in favor of focusing on buildings that actually contain and support human activity. Also not represented here are the myriad parks and boulevards that so splendidly define much of the area's civic infrastructure. Those deserve a volume of their own.

This project has been a labor of love for everyone involved with it. Long hours, passionate debate, and much objective thought, respect and delight have gone into this guidebook. We invite you to use and enjoy it.

Tom Bean, AIA
President,
AIA/KC 2000

Bryan Gross, AIA
Chairman,
AIA/KC
Guidebook Committee

# Public Art in Kansas City

LIKE MANY CITIES IN THE UNITED STATES, KANSAS CITY HAD A PUBLIC ART ordinance on the books long before 1991, when city officials set aside a mandated one percent from construction costs of municipal buildings in order to commission art. Also similar to other cities' efforts, this action was not taken lightly. On the contrary, it provoked heated debate. Some citizens believed that Kansas City's long-standing tradition of civic-minded patrons privately commissioning or purchasing art to adorn the city's urban spaces, splendid parks, and public places — like the venerated J.C. Nichols' Country Club Plaza — was a sufficient response to the demand for public art.

To the credit of numerous dedicated community leaders, patrons, and an expansive arts community, today, almost a decade after the implementation of Kansas City's One-Percent-for-Art Program, both private and public commissions flourish in Kansas City. Together, these publicly and privately supported efforts have forged an extraordinary vision for public art in Kansas City, distinguishable from any other city, and worthy of the national attention it has received.

The public art works included in this publication were intentionally limited to those works commissioned from contemporary artists working in relationship to architecture and site. In making these selections, the jury of Kansas City architectural professionals who evaluated the book's content took into consideration both the context of this publication and the numerous publications that already exist to attest to the rich tradition of fountains, monuments, and traditional sculpture in Kansas City. In addition, in order to encourage driving tours of the city's architecture and public art, only those works located outdoors are featured.

These stipulations aside, the public works featured in this publication are a testament to the expanding vision of the Kansas City community. A monumental public work, R.M. Fisher's *Sky Stations,* commissioned by the city's One-Percent-for-Art Program and installed by helicopter in 1994, made an indelible mark on Kansas City's skyscape. Other works included here are easily recognized as some of the best work of nationally renowned artists, such as Claes Oldenburg and Coosje van Bruggen's *Shuttlecocks*. These giant fiberglass sculptures redefined the neoclassical façade and lawn of the Nelson-Atkins Museum of Art when they were acquired through the Sosland Family for the museum in 1994.

*Sky Stations, Shuttlecocks* and other works of public art pushed previously held standards for taste and appropriateness farther than ever before in Kansas City. The rewards, as evidenced by the reproductions of these colossal sculptures on everything from telephone book covers, to television news backdrops, to national publications and media spots, have themselves been larger than life.

Public art in Kansas City has come a remarkably long way since the publication of an architectural guidebook in 1979. Since then, patrons and artists alike have taken seriously the task of commissioning and creating art that seeks a meaningful relationship to architecture, site, and finally, community. The 2000 guidebook would be remiss if it excluded an exciting development in the region's built environment: the large number of art works created over the last two decades that cohabit with architecture. For example, Jonathan Borofsky's *Walking Man* can be spotted on top of the COM Building on the Johnson County Community College campus, and Dale Eldred's realization of Frank Lloyd Wright's vision of a *Light Steeple* can be seen at night streaming heavenward from the Community Christian Church on Main Street.

Such works became far more than enhancements to buildings. They became expressions of the region's creative energy, embedded in the consciousness of the community, and crucial to the spirit of this place, our Kansas City.

Blair Sands
Public Art Administrator,
Municipal Art Commission,
City of Kansas City, Missouri

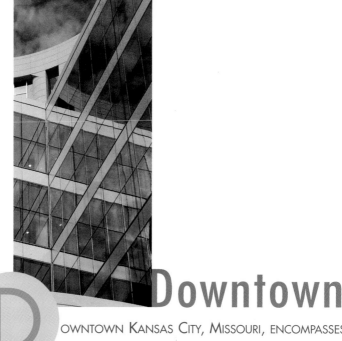

# Downtown

OWNTOWN KANSAS CITY, MISSOURI, ENCOMPASSES an area extending from the Missouri River to 31st Street and east from State Line Road to Troost Avenue.

During the late 1860s, this area began to interest merchants and residents when Kersey Coates, a real estate speculator, began investing in and developing the land around what is now 10th Street. South of the original center of commerce, the Riverfront District, the Coates Addition was platted. The new development attracted wealthy families to build mansions on the bluffs overlooking the river, a neighborhood that came to be known as Quality Hill. The Coates Hotel was built in 1891 and encouraged growth along Broadway.

Around the same time, the property east of Quality Hill along Ninth Street was developing. It became known as "The Junction," the busiest financial, social and cultural district in the city. Major Samuel D. Vaughn hired Asa Beebe Cross, a prominent Kansas City architect, to design "Vaughn's Diamond," a flatiron building at the convergence of Ninth, Main and Delaware streets.

During the 1870s and 1880s, construction of new buildings in downtown Kansas City, Missouri, increased, though most of the land in the city nicknamed "Gully Town" was marked by high bluffs and deep ravines. Over time, the bluffs were cut down more than 60 feet to accommodate zealous commercial and residential builders. In the 1880s, Kansas City's population more than doubled and the city stretched to 13 square miles. Imposing structures such as the New England Building and the New York Life Building, the city's first high-rise, were designed by prestigious architectural firms and constructed during this time.

After the city graded and paved Grand Avenue, a project that involved cutting out 30 to 40 feet of hilltop, the Central Business District experienced a huge building boom. Many steel-frame skyscrapers were built, including the 14-story office building at 10th Street and Grand Avenue, and the Scarritt Building. New construction yielded three of the country's most prized Art Deco skyscrapers and continued through the 1930s in spite of the Great Depression.

Following World War II, Quality Hill began to decline and many single-family dwellings disappeared from the area. Though the Central Business District has remained the center of business in Kansas City, Missouri, and has seen the construction of many new buildings, the migration away from the heart of the city in the 1950s continued as suburbs began to offer the same services. Recently, government incentives have encouraged restoration and redevelopment projects like those in Quality Hill and the River Market in an effort to revitalize the urban core and attract more businesses and residents to move to historic downtown.

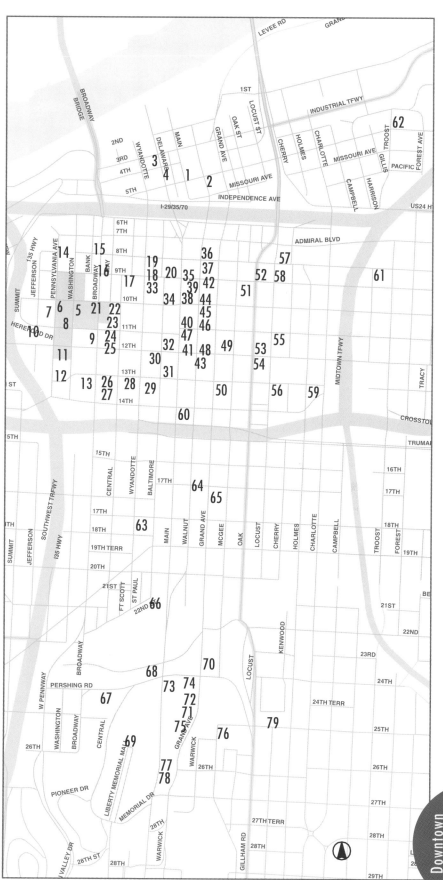

1 CITY MARKET, FIFTH AND WALNUT STREETS, 1940, FREDERICK C. GUNN; RENOVATION, 1991, DUNCAN ARCHITECTS, INC. Located near the site where fur trader François Chouteau built the first Kansas City trading post, the City Market has been an open-air market since the 1850s. Built in 1939 as part of Kansas City's "Ten-Year Plan" to create jobs and renovated in 1991, these buff-colored buildings support a Saturday farmers' market, a Sunday arts and crafts market and many shops, restaurants and community events.

2 HORTON'S OYSTER AND CHOP HOUSE, 507 WALNUT STREET, 1879, ARCHITECT UNKNOWN. Located in the River Market area, this restaurant enjoyed huge popularity with early Kansas City businessmen. Its peaked roof, pressed metal entablature, checkerboard brick, and multi-paned windows enliven its façade.

# Historic River Market

Extending from the Missouri River to Fifth Street, the HISTORIC RIVER MARKET can be described as the birthplace of Kansas City. The location of one of the most accessible river landing sites, the area became the first commercial center in Kansas City and is the site of the present City Market. Over the years, Kansas Citians such as Wild Bill Hickok, Wyatt Earp, Tom Pendergast and William Rockhill Nelson owned businesses in the district.

**3** DELAWARE STREET, SECOND TO FIFTH STREETS. This is one of the few remaining commercial streetscapes from late 19th century downtown Kansas City. In the beginning, Delaware developed a bit more slowly than Main Street, but eventually became the hub of business exchange for decades. Many structures display fine architectural form and details such as Romanesque arches, intricate cornice brickwork, cast-iron columns and stained glass.

**4** PACIFIC HOUSE HOTEL, 401 DELAWARE STREET, 1860, REBUILT 1868, ASA BEEBE CROSS; RENOVATION, 1999. Designed by one of Kansas City's early architects, this building features a cast-iron arcade. Considered the city's finest hotel until the late 1880s, the hotel's guests included Jesse James. Union Army troops occupied the hotel during the Civil War and it was the site where General Thomas Ewing issued the infamous Order No. 11, banishing more than 20,000 Confederate sympathizers from their homes and the city.

**5** QUALITY HILL, 12-BLOCK DOWNTOWN AREA WEST OF BROADWAY AND MAIN STREET, 1856-1929; REDEVELOPMENT, 1988, PGAV ARCHITECTS. Quality Hill, a fashionable neighborhood near the Central Business District, was developed in the late 19th century on land originally owned by Kersey Coates. Prominent citizens built large residences here but the development of the meat-packing industry railroads and stockyards in the West Bottoms reduced the desirability of the residential neighborhood. By the end of World War II, the area needed renewal and many of the original residences were removed and replaced by large office and apartment structures. As time wore on, downtown deterioration and lack of adequate housing did little to attract new residents and visitors to the Central Business District.

In March 1986, McCormack Baron and Associates of St. Louis and PGAV Architects introduced the $40 million Quality Hill Redevelopment Project. Phase I of the project provided nearly 250 new and renovated housing units in 11 historic buildings and more than 11,000 square feet of infill townhouses. The project immediately won public acclaim and emphasized how careful rehabilitation can dramatically change and revive the urban core. After Quality Hill was accepted as an historic district on the National Register in 1978, it became possible to rehabilitate this area and, in the process, help the effort for downtown revitalization. The design utilizes historic materials, massing and forms, consistent streetscaping and landscaping.

6 RESIDENCE, MAJOR WILLIAM WARNER, 1021 PENNSYLVANIA AVENUE, 1868, ARCHITECT UNKNOWN; RESTORATION, 1966, MONROE AND LEFEBRE ARCHITECTS, INC. Located in Quality Hill, the Warner residence is a prime example of early Kansas City residential architecture. In 1966, the structure was restored by the owners and earned the Urban Design Award from the Municipal Art Commission. The restoration helped spark the revitalization of the Quality Hill area.

7 RESIDENCE, GEORGE BLOSSOM, 1032 PENNSYLVANIA AVENUE, 1888, VAN BRUNT AND HOWE. This elegant residence constructed of brick with terra cotta trim and sandstone lintels and sills is one of the few remaining grand houses in the Quality Hill area. The residential space includes a courtyard and carriage house. A stone wall surrounds the property.

8 THE VIRGINIA HOTEL/HISTORIC HEART OF AMERICA UNITED WAY CORPORATE HEADQUARTERS, 1080 WASHINGTON, 1877-1890, THOMAS CORRIGAN; RENOVATION, 1990, GOULD EVANS ASSOCIATES. Originally the historic Virginia Hotel, this complex is composed of three buildings including two 1877 Italianate-style homes that are connected by a third structure built in 1890. Restoration involved total renovation of the interior and the construction of a large atrium, which connects the buildings.

9 CATHEDRAL OF THE IMMACULATE CONCEPTION, 411 W. 10TH STREET, 1882, T.R. TINSLEY; RENOVATION, 1960, MACKEY & ROARK, AND SHAUGHNESSY, BOWER AND GRIMALDI. Catholics have held this site since 1834 when Father Benedict Roux, pastor of the Chouteau settlement, purchased the land for $6 and built "Chouteau's Church." In 1857, 300 Irish laborers traveled to Kansas City to build the second church on the site and many of them stayed in town. When the church was renovated in 1960, 23-carat gold leaf was applied to the original copper dome and spire to prevent deterioration. The bright dome is a highly visible image on Kansas City's skyline.

**10** AMERICAN HEREFORD ASSOCIATION BUILDING, 715 W. 11TH STREET (HEREFORD DRIVE), 1951, JOSEPH RADOTINSKY; RENOVATION AND ADDITION, 1995, CDFM² ARCHITECTURE; ADDITION, 2000, HNTB ARCHITECTS. Built during a period of urban renewal in Quality Hill as the headquarters for an agribusiness organization, this structure was very modern for its time. A Hereford bull form, a recognizable symbol of Kansas City and its rich cattle industry history, sits atop a tower in front of the building.

**11** 1220 WASHINGTON OFFICE BUILDING, 1220 WASHINGTON STREET, 1987, PBNI ARCHITECTS. Designed as a headquarters facility, this three-story, circular building features brick, limestone and copper as does the building's free-standing, two-level parking garage.

**12** ARGUS BUILDING, 1300 WASHINGTON, 1997, GOULD EVANS GOODMAN ASSOCIATES. This L-shaped structure is designed to emphasize its "gateway" location. The 85,000 square-foot building has a façade that consists of brick, metal panels and a sunscreen cornice.

**13** GRACE AND HOLY TRINITY CATHEDRAL, 415 W. 13TH STREET, CHURCH, 1887-1890, NAVE, 1894, FREDERICK E. HILL; GUILDHALL, 1889, ADRIANCE VAN BRUNT; TOWER, 1938, WIGHT AND WIGHT; COURTYARD ADDITION, 1981, ABEND SINGLETON ASSOCIATES; FELLOWSHIP HALL, 1994, GOULD EVANS ASSOCIATES AND TAYLOR MCDOUGALL BURNS ARCHITECTS. Begun as a mission of the St. Mary's Episcopal Church, this church has evolved into one of the area's largest Episcopal parishes. The three-story coursed and cut-stone church complex displays elements of Norman Gothic design including the square tower, semi-conical nave, masonry construction and tile roof. The 17,000 square-foot social hall and courtyard additions feature limestone walls, clay tile roofing, and custom steel doors and windows that complement the Cathedral's historic nave and bell tower.

Downtown

13

**14** INVESTORS FIDUCIARY TRUST COMPANY, 801 PENNSYLVANIA AVENUE, 1997, BNIM ARCHITECTS/CDFM² ARCHITECTURE. Occupying an imposing hilltop site near the spot where Lewis and Clark surveyed the Missouri River in 1804, this building creates a link between the Garment District and Quality Hill. Annodized aluminum columns rise from the fifth floor. A projecting sunscreen cornice and low parapet cap the building.

**15** COMMERCIAL BUILDINGS, 306-423 W. EIGHTH STREET, 1899-1909. The design of these buildings derives from the Chicago School of commercial architecture. At the turn of the century, Eighth Street was an extremly busy area for wholesale markets. Recent efforts to revitalize the west side of downtown have filled the previously vacant buildings with offices and residential lofts.

**16** POINDEXTER AND GATLIN OFFICE BUILDING, 330 W. NINTH STREET, 1901 (POINDEXTER), 1910 (GATLIN), ORIGINAL ARCHITECTS UNKNOWN; RENOVATION, 1997, BNIM ARCHITECTS/CDFM² ARCHITECTURE. Located in the historic Garment District of downtown Kansas City, the Poindexter and Gatlin Buildings evolved from two turn-of-the-century warehouses into one innovative office facility. Structural modifications to the Gatlin Building were necessary to align its floors with those of the Poindexter. The connected buildings now feature a new glass entrance. The south façade consists of pre-cast concrete and brick panels reminiscent of the original masonry.

**17** SAVOY HOTEL AND THE SAVOY GRILL RESTAURANT, 219 W. NINTH STREET, 1888, SIMEON CHAMBERLAIN; ADDITIONS, 1888-1906, VAN BRUNT AND HOWE; HOWE, HOIT AND CUTLER. Located on the edge of the early business district and restored in the 1960s, this elegant hotel retains original features such as imported marble, tile, claw-footed tubs, brass fixtures and stained glass windows. The lobby exhibits a magnificent Art Nouveau skylight. Over the years, the hotel has served such celebrities as Teddy Roosevelt, William Howard Taft, W.C. Fields, Will Rogers, Sara Bernhardt and John D. Rockefeller. Added in 1903, the Savoy Grill is Kansas City's oldest continuously operating restaurant. The restaurant boasts stained glass windows, an enormous oak bar and "Booth No. 4," which was reserved for President Harry S. Truman whenever he stayed at the Savoy.

**18** NEW ENGLAND BUILDING, 112 W. NINTH STREET, 1887, BRADLEE, WINSLOW AND WETHERELL, BOSTON. A result of the substantial Kansas City development boom in the late 1800s, this U-plan structure was commissioned by an eastern financial institution. This building is possibly the first fireproof construction in Kansas City.

**19** BUNKER BUILDING, 820 BALTIMORE AVENUE, 1881, ARCHITECT UNKNOWN. This Victorian/eclectic-style building was named after Walter A. Bunker, founder of the Western Newspaper Union, which occupied the building for many years. Located in the city's late 19th century business and financial center, this rectangular corner structure features limestone foundations and cast-iron columns.

# Ninth Street Historic District

The NINTH STREET HISTORIC DISTRICT was placed on the National Register of Historic Places in 1976. Buildings in this area formed the business and financial center of Kansas City in the late 19th century. At the turn of the 20th century, it was a favored place for realtors and architects to locate their offices.

**20** NEW YORK LIFE BUILDING, 20 W. NINTH, 1890, MCKIM, MEAD AND WHITE; RENOVATION, 1996, GASTINGER WALKER HARDEN ARCHITECTS. One of several buildings that the New York Life Insurance Company commissioned simultaneously in cities around the nation, this structure reflected the growing architectural interest in Renaissance Revival and, at 10 stories, it was considered Kansas City's first skyscraper. Extravagant terra cotta ornament and brickwork flank the upper façade and an eagle sculpture by Louis Saint-Gaudens sits above the entrance. Interior features include outstanding tile work that was completed by Russian immigrants. James Knapp, a carpenter who worked on the building, noted in 1936 that "common labor on this building drew $1.50 per day ... [and] carpenters $2.25 for 10 hours." In 1996, this Kansas City landmark was renovated to accommodate UtiliCorp United. Renovations included the addition of a new 600-vehicle parking garage and state-of-the-art energy, communications and environmental capabilities.

Downtown

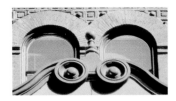

**21** COATES HOUSE HOTEL AND APARTMENTS, 1005 BROADWAY, 1886-1891, VAN BRUNT AND HOWE; RENOVATION, 1987, PGAV ARCHITECTS. Built on what was originally a cow pasture, the hotel was used by Union troops and hosted many well-known people such as President Grover Cleveland and his new bride, and President Teddy Roosevelt. In 1978, most of the south wing was ruined by fire and the building was left empty. In 1979, the Historic Kansas City Foundation purchased the building to protect it from demolition and resold it to the Kansas City Redevelopment Authority. As part of the Quality Hill Redevelopment Plan, the hotel was salvaged and converted into 38 new apartments and commercial space in 1987.

**22** TEN CENTRAL CAR PARK, 1016 CENTRAL STREET, 1985, PBNI ARCHITECTS. This parking garage provides 410 parking spaces for several buildings in Quality Hill and the Central Business District. A recessed arcade provides a sheltered passageway for street-level retail shops and effectively widens the sidewalk to accommodate a row of trees. The design mimics the heavily rusticated limestone façade of the adjacent fire station building (c.1905) yet offers inset hubcaps as unique and fitting ornamentation.

**23** CENTRAL FIRE STATION (NOW CENTRAL EXCHANGE), 1020 CENTRAL STREET, 1905, GEORGE W. HUGGINS; RENOVATION, 1985, PBNI ARCHITECTS. Located between Quality Hill and the Central Business District, this Mannerist interpretation of a classical façade is unusual for a fire station. The structure is connected to a newer structure, Ten Central Car Park, which emulates the station's heavily rusticated limestone façade.

**24** 333 W. 11TH STREET, 1996, BNIM ARCHITECTS/CDFM² ARCHITECTURE. This is a 96,000 square-foot five-story office building constructed to house an expanding data processing company. The exterior façade consists of brick and pre-cast concrete panels that are reminiscent of the neighboring historic buildings.

Downtown

19

**25** STANDARD/FOLLY THEATER, 300 W. 12TH STREET, 1900, GUNN AND CURTISS; RENOVATION, 1981, PBNA ARCHITECTS. This is the city's oldest surviving stage theater. Entertainers including Al Jolson, Fannie Brice, Eddie Foy and Jack Dempsey performed in the Folly. The Palladian window on the main façade highlights the building's neoclassical style. A band of third-story windows, topped by a central arch, creates this feature. The surrounding ornamental brickwork enhances the Palladian motif, and the three arched entrances with central pillasters further reinforce it. In the 1970s it became a likely candidate for demolition and concerned Kansas Citians started the effort to save and rehabilitate it. The result was the restoration of the exterior and redesign of the interior to remove some modifications and add patron comfort and safety features and state-of-the-art lighting and sound systems. The renovation also added a new wing to house ticket windows, administrative offices and theatrical support spaces.

**26** H. ROE BARTLE EXPOSITION CENTER, 301 W. 13TH STREET, 1976, CONVENTION CENTER ASSOCIATES, A JOINT VENTURE OF SELIGSON ASSOCIATES, INC., HORNER AND BLESSING, C.F. MURPHY ASSOCIATES, CHICAGO, AND HNTB ARCHITECTS; CONVENTION CENTER EXPANSION, 1994, HNTB ARCHITECTS; CONFERENCE CENTER ADDITION, 1994, BNIM ARCHITECTS. Located in downtown Kansas City, these buildings contain nearly 650,000 square feet of usable space. The 1976 building is architecturally noteworthy for its structural system of steel trusses that frame directly onto triangular end-frames. Barges transported the huge triangles up the Missouri River because they were too heavy to be transported by highway. Voters approved a $100 million bond issue to expand the complex in 1989. Completed in 1994, the expansion included an enlarged exhibition hall, a grand lobby, meeting room space, a great hall, truck docks and a three-story conference and banquet structure. The exhibition hall, covered by a cable roof structure, bridges the Crosstown Freeway and the floors above the first level of the new conference center are suspended over the sidewalk.

**27** SKY STATIONS, R.M. FISCHER, 301 W. 13TH STREET, 1994, ALUMINUM AND STEEL, EACH APPROXIMATELY 24' X 15'. Located atop Bartle Hall, R.M. Fischer's aluminum sculptures were placed upon 200-foot pillar supports by helicopter and emanate light over a two-mile radius at night. Transforming Kansas City's skyline, these futuristic sculptures, modeled after the 1930s Art Deco style used for many area buildings, were commissioned as part of the Municipal Art Commission's One-Percent-For-Art Program.

Downtown

**28** MUNICIPAL AUDITORIUM, 211 W. 13TH STREET, 1934, GENTRY, VOSCAMP AND NEVILLE, AND HOIT, PRICE AND BARNES. Built as part of Kansas City's Ten-Year Plan, this enormous building contains an arena, music hall, small theater, exhibition hall and committee rooms that retain their original décor. Constructed during the Depression at a cost of $6.5 million, it was one of the best convention and entertainment facilities in the country and remains one of the premiere Art Deco buildings in the United States.

# Ten-Year Plan

With the help of "Boss Tom" Pendergast, the TEN-YEAR PLAN was passed by a 4-1 majority in 1931. The plan, a $40 million bond program, called for the increase of public works projects in order to assuage the effects of unemployment caused by the Great Depression. As a result, unemployment rates went down; City Hall, the Jackson County Courthouse and the Municipal Auditorium went up; and improvements to the Downtown Airport and the Kansas City Zoo were completed.

**29** KANSAS CITY POWER AND LIGHT CO. BUILDING, 1330 BALTIMORE AVENUE, 1931, HOIT, PRICE AND BARNES. This 36-story building is significant as one of the first Kansas City high-rises to embody architectural modernism. Its dramatic stepbacks and stylized geometric surface decoration are typical of Art Deco-style skyscrapers. Covered in Indiana limestone, each recessed step conceals floodlights, and the six-story crowning shaft features prismatic glass panels and alternating multicolored lights. Sunburst ornamental motifs adorn the exterior, symbolizing light and energy. This structure, the Municipal Auditorium, and the Jackson County Courthouse are thought to be three of the nation's Art Deco treasures.

**30** MUEHLEBACH HOTEL, 200 W. 12TH STREET, 1915, HOLABIRD AND ROCHE; RENOVATION AND ADDITION, 1997, BNIM ARCHITECTS. Located in the heart of downtown, this historic hotel has hosted many illustrious guests including Independence native President Harry S. Truman. In 1948, Truman awoke at the Muehlebach to find he had defied the forecasters and defeated Thomas Dewey for the presidency. Renovation of the hotel and the construction of a new 18-story tower addition occurred in 1997. The stone, terra cotta and brick exterior was repaired. The new tower elements include red granite columns, pre-cast concrete and brick materials to meld with the original structure.

**31** MIDLAND THEATER AND OFFICE BUILDING, 1228-1234 MAIN AND 1221-23 BALTIMORE AVENUE, 1927, THOMAS W. LAMB; RENOVATIONS 1988, 1998, THEODORE KNAPP/TK ARCHITECTS, CRAIG PATTERSON AND ASSOCIATES, AND BNIM ARCHITECTS. Designed by one of the nation's premiere theater architects, the Midland complex includes a 12-story office building and a six-story, 4,000-seat theater. Built to house silent movies and live entertainment, it was the grandest movie palace in the city and the third largest theater in the nation at the time of construction. The 1988 renovations included renewing the terra cotta façade, the east window and the lavish, French Baroque and Rococo interiors and replacing the marquee. In 1998, street level retail shops and the theater entrance were restored to their original 1920s appearance.

**32** ONE KANSAS CITY PLACE, 1200 MAIN, 1988, PBNI ARCHITECTS. This commanding 42-story, 1.3 million square-foot retail and office building follows the city's tall-building heritage while also offering its own interpretation of that tradition. The exterior of the building utilizes a tinted glass skin accented by vertical granite strips and clear glazed corners to emphasize the building's setbacks.

**33** UNION CARBIDE BUILDING, 912 BALTIMORE AVENUE, 1931, WILLIAM A. BOVARD. The geometric foliate terra cotta panels that decorate the stepped cornice and first two stories express the Art Deco styling of this 11-story building.

Downtown

**34** First National Bank Building, 14 W. 10th Street, 1904-1906, Wilder and Wight; east annex, 1926, Wight and Wight. An imposing neoclassical structure with oversized marble columns and terra cotta capitals, this building's Chicago-style windows with metal mullions form a curtain wall between the columns, which is unusual for the imposing style. The interior has been restored and retains its original elegant gold and white neoclassical décor.

**35** Commerce Tower, 911 Main Street, 1965, Keene and Simpson and Murphy. This 30-story curtain-wall office façade is constructed of pre-cast stone panels that provide the framework for a geometric pattern of glass on the upper levels. At street level, the building features a glass-enclosed interior corridor system and an outside terrace and garden.

**36** GUMBEL BUILDING, 801 WALNUT, 1904, JOHN W. MCKECKNIE; RENOVATION, 1984, GOULD EVANS ASSOCIATES. This is a very early example of a reinforced concrete office building. The structure features fine terra cotta detail, neoclassical sculpture and the tripartite windows made famous by the Chicago School architects. While its exquisite exterior was in good condition, in 1984 this 50,000 square-foot office building required complete replacement of all major building systems and the creation of a modern meeting room.

**37** SCARRITT BUILDING AND SCARRITT ARCADE, 818 GRAND AVENUE, 819 WALNUT STREET, 1907, ROOT AND SIEMENS; RENOVATION, 1985, SOLOMON CLAYBOUGH YOUNG. An under-alley connects the 11-story steel-framed Scarritt Building to the adjoining four-story arcade. The terra cotta ornament at the pedestrian level and cornice of both buildings are an outstanding expression of Sullivan-esque design.

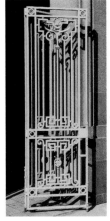

**38** COMMERCE TRUST BUILDING, 922 WALNUT STREET, 1908, JARVIS HUNT; RENOVATION, 2000, GASTINGER WALKER HARDEN ARCHITECTS. This 16-story granite, brick and terra cotta building houses one of Missouri's largest banks. Connected to the Commerce Tower by an interior corridor and escalators, the building's exterior features three prominent arches and ornate relief.

**39** COMMERCE BANK BUILDING, 1000 WALNUT STREET, 1985, HELLMUTH, OBATA & KASSABAUM, INC. Linked to the Commerce Tower and Commerce Trust Buildings by skywalk, this 19-story, 477,000 square-foot structure is characterized by dramatic stepbacks, clear and bronze reflecting glass and a standing seam copper roof. It houses office spaces, a shopping arcade, an art gallery and a 650-car parking garage. The $45 million building also features reinforced concrete supports and a polished granite façade.

**40** AT&T TOWN PAVILION, 1100 WALNUT STREET, 1987, HNTB ARCHITECTS. This 38-story, 1.2 million square-foot office and retail complex features a barrel-vaulted, five-story rotunda in its retail area. The Pavilion provides space for more than 70 retail shops and restaurants as well as a food court.

**41** BOLEY CLOTHING COMPANY BUILDING, 1124-1130 WALNUT STREET, 1909, LOUIS S. CURTISS. The work of one of Kansas City's most famous, innovative and idiosyncratic architects, this six-story building is renowned as one of the first glass curtain-wall structures in the world. The building features terra cotta ornaments, iron detailing and cantilevered floor slabs.

**42** FIDELITY NATIONAL BANK AND TRUST CO., 911 WALNUT STREET, 1931, HOIT, PRICE AND BARNES. This 36-story building has a stylized neoclassical exterior that combines 1930s geometric styling with pilasters and classical capitals. A pair of short towers adorns the top of the building and the surface is decorated with a wealth of stylized vegetal motifs of glazed terra cotta.

**43** 1201 WALNUT BUILDING, 1201 WALNUT STREET, 1991, HNTB ARCHITECTS. The 30-story office building uses a sophisticated curtain wall that incorporates granite panels with gray-blue glazing and black accents. The building, which sits atop a parking garage, connects directly to Kansas City's skywalk system via the building's multi-story lobby.

**44** UNITED MISSOURI BANK HEADQUARTERS, 1010 GRAND AVENUE, 1986, ABEND SINGLETON ASSOCIATES. This building has a two-story granite colonnade and simple ornamental detail. A pedestrian alley leads into a central courtyard, which features a curving granite and stainless steel staircase, a fountain, and *KC Harvester,* a colorful sculpture by Nancy Graves.

**45** *KC HARVESTER,* NANCY GRAVES, 1010 GRAND AVENUE, 1987, BRONZE, STAINLESS STEEL AND BLACK GRANITE, 18' x 12' x 5'5". Commissioned by United Missouri Bank, this sculpture is the focal point of the courtyard at the company's downtown headquarters. Painted bronze objects cast from stainless steel rise above the black granite base. The colorful sculpture depicts vegetation and objects found in the Midwest such as corn, wheat, sunflowers, a windmill, a tractor part and a rake.

Downtown

**46** BRYANT BUILDING, 1102 GRAND AVENUE, 1931, GRAHAM, ANDERSON, PROBST AND WHITE, CHICAGO. This Art Deco office tower is 26 stories high. The exterior features setbacks, recessed spandrels and a variety of materials including contiguous lines of white glazed brick and dark terra cotta that accentuate the building's verticality.

**47** MERCANTILE BANK, 1101 WALNUT STREET, 1974, HARRY A. WEESE AND ASSOCIATES, CHICAGO. This unusual building in downtown Kansas City displays the structural expressiveness of 1970s architecture. Resting atop steel columns, this tall steel and glass curtain-wall skyscraper features bronze reflecting glass and large triangular trusses angling out from its base.

**48** BONFILS BUILDING, 1200 GRAND AVENUE, 1925, FREDERICK C. GUNN; RENOVATION, 1988, ABEND SINGLETON ASSOCIATES. Frederick G. Bonfils, publisher of *The Kansas City Journal* from 1909 to 1922, commissioned this two-story structure. It is in the Venetian Renaissance Revival style and features a terra cotta façade manufactured to imitate finely cut ashlar stone.

**49** CURTISS STUDIO BUILDING, 1118-1120 McGEE STREET, 1909, LOUIS S. CURTISS. The second of his signature glass curtain-wall structures located downtown, this building housed Curtiss himself on the third floor in exotic living quarters, which featured a rooftop courtyard off his bedroom.

**50** MISSOURI COURT OF APPEALS, 1300 McGEE STREET, 1983, ABEND SINGLETON ASSOCIATES. Located near Kansas City's major governmental buildings, this structure features an enormous glass and masonry vault. The monumental limestone portal nobly frames the entrance and 11 arched windows indicate the judges' chambers.

**51** COMMERCIAL BUILDING, 924-26 OAK STREET, 1912, JOHN W. McKECKNIE. Originally built for the undertaking firm of Stine and McClure, this building incorporates the Egyptian Revival style. McKecknie, a leading Kansas City architect of the time, considered his clients' needs and chose a style that has traditionally held funerary connotations.

**52** CHARLES EVANS WHITTAKER U.S. COURTHOUSE, 400 E. NINTH STREET, 1998, ELLERBE BECKET/ASAI ARCHITECTS. This crescent-shaped building at the north end of the Civic Mall houses judges' chambers, court-related agencies, multimedia conference facilities, a cafeteria, 21 courtrooms and enclosed parking for 100 vehicles. The 600,000 square-foot, 10-story building features a central glass-lined rotunda lobby, a spectacular entryway, and vertical windows that provide security and a broad view of the bluffs and the Missouri River.

**53** CITY HALL, 414 E. 12TH STREET, 1937, WIGHT AND WIGHT ARCHITECTS. The ornament and form of this skyscraper's interior and limestone exterior are in Classical Moderne and Art Deco styles. In the elaborate lobby, detailed friezes portray various professions, and the city's seal is set into the floor. Images on the bronze elevator doors illustrate the modes of transportation that helped Kansas City flourish, and bronze panels in the Council Chambers pay homage to the city's agricultural heritage.

**54** JACKSON COUNTY COURTHOUSE, 415 E. 12TH STREET, 1934, WIGHT AND WIGHT ARCHITECTS, KEENE AND SIMPSON, AND FREDERICK C. GUNN. Supported by the power of political boss Tom Pendergast and encouraged by Harry S. Truman, who was a Jackson County Judge, this skyscraper was built in the Art Deco style. Forming a visual unit with City Hall, its box-like base supports a tower that has vertical panels of windows and spandrels. Above the sixth floor, a horizontal frieze depicts Kansas City history.

**55** MODERN COMMUNICATION, TERRY ALLEN, 12TH AND CHERRY STREETS, 1995, BRONZE, 77.5" x 41" x 21". This bronze statue depicts a businessman standing atop his briefcase with his eyes covered by his tie, his fingers in his ears, and a shoe in his mouth. Standing in a busy downtown courtyard, the arresting sculpture encourages diverse interpretation.

**56** SHADOW GARDEN, STEVE WHITACRE, JACKSON COUNTY JAIL EXPANSION, 1300 CHERRY STREET, 1998, BRONZE, BRICK, AND LIVE FOLIAGE, 18' x 128' x 65'. Focusing on the psychology of confinement, Whitacre uses trees, ground cover and bronze linear elements to create a sculptural statement of nature incarcerated. The piece emulates a jail cell through its lack of space and privacy. The foliage, as prisoner, is both bound by the brick wall and yet free to grow through the cage-like framework.

Downtown

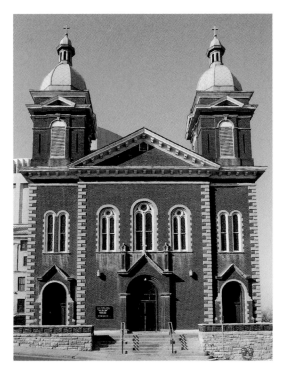

**57** ST. PATRICK'S CATHEDRAL, 800 CHERRY STREET, 1875, ASA BEEBE CROSS. Designed by one of the earliest and busiest Kansas City architects, this building utilizes the Italianate style. The Catholic parishioners who commissioned the church also made the bricks and did the bricklaying.

**58** PUBLIC LIBRARY BUILDING, 500 E. NINTH STREET, 1897, WILLIAM F. HACKNEY AND ADRIANCE VAN BRUNT; ADDITION, 1918, CHARLES A. SMITH; RENOVATION, 1985, SOLOMON CLAYBOUGH YOUNG. Commissioned by the school board and encouraged by local interest in the "City Beautiful" movement, this building is indicative of the cultural and political growth of 19th century Kansas City. One of the few Second Renaissance Revival-style buildings remaining in the city, its exterior cornice displays various authors' names and the interior contains opulent marble columns, pedestals and a grand fireplace in the lobby.

**59** St. Mary's Episcopal Church, 1307 Holmes, 1888, William Halsey Wood. Built in a neighborhood that was originally residential, this is one of the few remaining churches in the Central Business District. An excellent example of Victorian Gothic Revival-style architecture, this structure is noteworthy for its painted marble altar and its beautiful stained glass windows. This church was known as "the mother parish of Kansas City" and established the mission church that is now the Grace and Holy Trinity Cathedral on 13th Street.

**60** Kansas City Division of Employment Security Building, 1411 Main Street, 1967, Shaughnessy, Bower and Grimaldi. The contrasting exterior textures and spaces define the Brutalist style of this four-story reinforced concrete structure.

**61** Covenant Baptist Church, 821 Harrison Street, 1888, Edbrooke and Burnham, Chicago; reconstruction, 1949, architect unknown. This Romanesque building boasts excellent stonework and ornamental entablature. A 1949 fire destroyed the towering gable roof though the heavily rusticated first-story and semi-circular arches of the original design remain. During the 1880s and 1890s, Daniel Burnham was a visionary architect in Chicago and was responsible for major urban projects including the Chicago Columbian Exposition.

**62** Garrison Community Center, 1124 E. Fifth Street, 1913, Ben J. Lubschez of A. Van Brunt and Co. Open to the public, this multi-use building mimics the style of Perkins' early designs for the Chicago public school system.

**63** MOVIE HOUSE ROW, 18TH AND WYANDOTTE STREETS AND SURROUNDING AREA. From 1902 to 1958, an unusual mixture of buildings associated with the film industry were designed and built here by various architects including Clarence Kivett and John McKecknie. Theater and film studios including Warner Brothers, Metro-Goldwyn-Mayer, Paramount, Fox, and Durwood Theaters had offices in the neighborhood. Many of the buildings, constructed in the 1930s and 1940s, express the era and their association with film through modern architectural styling.

**64** TAYLOR BUILDING, 1701 WALNUT, 1902, ARCHITECT UNKNOWN. This Renaissance Revival-style building features finely detailed brickwork and stone ornament including the Palladian motifs on the third-story windows and decoration inspired by the Chicago architect Louis H. Sullivan.

Downtown

41

**65** THE KANSAS CITY STAR BUILDING, 1729 GRAND AVENUE, 1911, JARVIS HUNT, CHICAGO. William Rockhill Nelson, co-founder of *The Kansas City Star*, commissioned Hunt to design this printing facility. Directed by Nelson to base his design on the McLean Residence in Washington, D.C., Hunt created this Italianate Renaissance-style structure rich in surface decoration.

**66** CHICAGO, MILWAUKEE, AND ST. PAUL RAILROAD DEPOT, 101-102 W. 22ND STREET, 1888, ARCHITECT UNKNOWN; RENOVATION, 1998, SHAW HOFSTRA + ASSOCIATES. Built as a freight depot for the Chicago, Milwaukee, and St. Paul Railroad, the building is constructed of brick with a gable roof, multiple segmental arched windows and overhead freight doors. Recent renovations were made to house a series of destination restaurants and include the addition of interior dividing infrastructure, brick sidewalks, custom light fixtures, sculptures, landscaping and a terrace. This is one of a number of renovations in the area that have sparked a rebirth of the Crossroads district.

# Crossroads District

By the 1890s, Kansas City's booming economy was severely overtaxing the city's West Bottoms rail facilities. As an alternative to the established but strained West Bottoms, two small freight depots built south of downtown in the late 1880s encouraged the construction of rail-dependent factories and warehouses in this area, known as the CROSSROADS DISTRICT. These buildings were of masonry and reinforced concrete construction with stone and metal trim highlighting their simple brick façades. Construction of Union Station in 1914 solidified the economy of this area and encouraged further industrial and commercial development.

**67** POST OFFICE BUILDING, 315 W. PERSHING ROAD, 1933, JAMES WETMORE. Built in only 17 months, this was the first of many major government structures to be financed and built under the Ten-Year Plan. The structure was linked by tunnel to Union Station's railroad baggage levels.

**68** UNION STATION, 30 W. PERSHING ROAD, 1910-1914, JARVIS HUNT, CHICAGO; RENOVATION, 1999, DESIGN ARCHITECTS: EHRENKRANTZ, ECKSTUT & KUHN, NEW YORK, AND KEYES CONDON & FLORANCE, WASHINGTON, D.C.; PROJECT ARCHITECTS: UNION STATION ARCHITECTS, A CONSORTIUM OF HNTB ARCHITECTS, BNIM ARCHITECTS, CDFM$^2$ ARCHITECTURE, MACKEY MITCHELL ZAHNER, AND RAFAEL ARCHITECTS; PRESERVATION ARCHITECT: OEHRLEIN & ASSOCIATES. A product of the "City Beautiful" movement, this beaux-arts style structure was built to replace the old Union Depot (c.1878). Unlike many terminals, the structure was designed for trains to actually pass through it. Its innovative design consisted of six stories with separate levels for passengers, waiting rooms and baggage. The third largest station in the world when it was built, it faced demolition in 1971 when tentative plans to build a 54-acre business complex on the site were announced because use of the station had diminished. In 1983, only the Amtrak passenger waiting room, an inflatable bubble inside the Grand Hall, remained active. The station was permanently closed in 1989 and maintenance ceased. In 1996, an historic bistate cultural tax initiative, the first such public financing effort in the nation to bridge state lines, passed and provided $118 million to restore the historic Union Station and to construct a massive new educational museum, Science City, as an addition to the station. The redevelopment project, which cost an estimated $254 million, involved fully refurbishing the Station's Grand Hall and adding other attractions such as the interactive science museum, three theaters and restaurants. Union Station reopened in November 1999.

**69** LIBERTY MEMORIAL, 100 W. 26TH STREET, 1926, H. VAN BUREN MCGONIGLE, NEW YORK. This is the world's largest and America's only memorial dedicated to the fallen soldiers of World War I. The design was selected through a national architectural competition and the project was funded through public subscription. The complex includes the 217-foot Memorial Tower with sculptures symbolizing courage, honor, patriotism and sacrifice; two museum buildings containing the names of Kansas City soldiers who died in the war; the Great Frieze, depicting the timeline of the war; courtyards and staircases linking the structures; and the memorial wall featuring bronze busts of the five Allied leaders who were present for the groundbreaking in 1921. The completed memorial was dedicated by President Calvin Coolidge on Armistice Day in 1926. In 1998, Kansas Citians passed a tax initiative that provided $30 million for the memorial's restoration and $14.7 million for future maintenance.

**70** MUTUAL BENEFIT LIFE INSURANCE COMPANY BUILDING/IBM PLAZA AT CROWN CENTER, 2345 GRAND AVENUE, 1977, OFFICE OF MIES VAN DER ROHE, CHICAGO. Emulating 1960s design features, this 27-story glass box is constructed of steel covered by a cladding of anodized aluminum and solar glass. Part of the Crown Center plan, this building played a large role in the effort to visually transform the area around Pershing Road and Grand Avenue.

**71** CROWN CENTER, 25TH STREET AND GRAND AVENUE, 1970-1978, MASTER PLANNER AND COORDINATING ARCHITECT, EDWARD LARRABEE BARNES. Begun by Joyce C. Hall, founder of Hallmark Cards, this residential, business and commercial development is located on 85 acres of previously blighted property known as Signboard Hill. Crown Center contains a shopping, dining and entertainment center, two million square feet of office space and the city's two largest hotels. During the winter the outdoor square is home to Kansas City's only public outdoor ice rink and the Mayor's Christmas Tree. The complex attracts a wide variety of visitors for festivals, concerts, shopping and conventions, serving tourists as well as Kansas City residents.

Downtown

47

**72** CROWN CENTER OFFICE/RETAIL COMPLEX, 2450 GRAND AVENUE, 1971-1973, EDWARD LARRABEE BARNES, NEW YORK, AND MARSHALL AND BROWN. This complex is composed of a series of five interconnected seven-story office buildings that are stair-stepped to follow the hill's natural sloping topography and overlook the court and lawn areas of Crown Center Square.

**73** CROWN CENTER HOTEL, ONE PERSHING ROAD, 1973, HARRY WEESE AND ASSOCIATES, CHICAGO, AND MARSHALL AND BROWN. The 15-story, L-shaped structure was built on Signboard Hill. The interior of the five-story lobby incorporates exposed sections of the hill and features a 60-foot waterfall carved into the natural limestone.

# Hallmark Cards Fine Art Collection

The HALLMARK CARDS FINE ART COLLECTION contains more than 3,500 pieces of art, including commissioned original paintings by Georgia O'Keefe and Norman Rockwell and outdoor sculpture by renowned sculptors such as Alexander Calder and Kenneth Snelson. Frequently, the art is loaned to museums for special exhibits and the on-site sculptures are colorful additions to Crown Center.

**74** *SHIVA*, ALEXANDER CALDER, ONE PERSHING ROAD, 1965, INSTALLED 1974, PAINTED STEEL, 22′ x 16′ x 18′. Located at the corner of Pershing Road and Grand Avenue, this red-painted, four-armed steel sculpture represents the Hindu mythological god of destruction and reproduction. This stabile form was completely stripped and repainted in 1991.

**75** CROWN CENTER APARTMENTS, 2510 GRAND AVENUE, AND 2525 MAIN STREET, 1976, THE ARCHITECTS' COLLABORATIVE, CAMBRIDGE, MASS., AND MARSHALL AND BROWN. Crown Center's residential component includes the San Francisco Tower, a 32-story condominium tower, and Santa Fe Place, an adjacent seven-story building with 110 rental units.

**76** HALLMARK CARDS, 25TH STREET AND MCGEE TRAFFICWAY, 1950-1955, WELTON BECKETT, LOS ANGELES. Headquarters to the world's largest personal greeting card company, this structure serves as an interesting, enormous office/industrial complex. A series of irregularly stacked boxes breaks up the rectangular mass of the structure.

**77** 2600 GRAND OFFICE BUILDING, 2600 GRAND AVENUE, 1991, PEI COBB FREED ARCHITECTS AND BNIM ARCHITECTS. Located at a prominent site at the intersection of Grand Avenue and Main Street, this 12-story office building is enhanced by granite horizontal banding. A sophisticated glazing system helps the building conserve energy and maintain optimal light levels.

**78** *TRIPLE CROWN*, KENNETH D. SNELSON, 2600 GRAND AVENUE, 1991, STAINLESS STEEL, 43' X 85' X 78'. Commissioned by Hallmark Cards, this sculpture features oversized solid stainless steel cylinders held in place by tension wires. The sculptor's intent was to represent "the multitude of contesting forces pushing and pulling at one another, all confined to a finite space with all parts independent."

**79** RONALD MCDONALD HOUSE, 2501 CHERRY STREET, 1988, PBNI ARCHITECTS. This structure is the nation's 100th Ronald McDonald House. Balancing private and communal spaces, the house provides a homelike atmosphere for out-of-town families of hospitalized children. The exterior mimics the architecture of nearby Kansas City-style shirtwaist dwellings with different cladding materials on the first and upper stories. The broad, overhanging eaves, large porches and expansive windows pay homage to the Arts and Crafts architectural style.

# Westside

BOUNDED BY THE MISSOURI RIVER, INTERSTATE Highway 35 and the Kansas River, the west side of Kansas City, Missouri, has a rich industrial and cultural history. The flat flood plains at the convergence of the Missouri and Kansas rivers provided a promising site for the development of the manufacturing, cattle and trade industries in what came to be known as the West Bottoms. The Hannibal Bridge (c.1869) produced the rail connections that made Kansas City the central point in the United States for transportation of goods and cattle. As a result, large red brick Romanesque-style factories and warehouses and large stockyards were built to service these industries. In the late 19th and early 20th centuries, Irish and Mexican immigrants lived in late Victorian-style rental houses that were built close to the warehouses and factories.

The West Bottoms has witnessed redevelopment projects such as the construction of Kemper Arena and the American Royal. Most recently, artists have begun transforming the old warehouses into studios and lofts.

Though the Westside neighborhood was divided, it experienced a rebirth in the 1970s and 1980s. Southwest Boulevard, the area's commercial strip, is a successful commercial center and reflects the Mexican-American heritage of its residents and showcases many of the city's oldest Victorian homes.

Westside

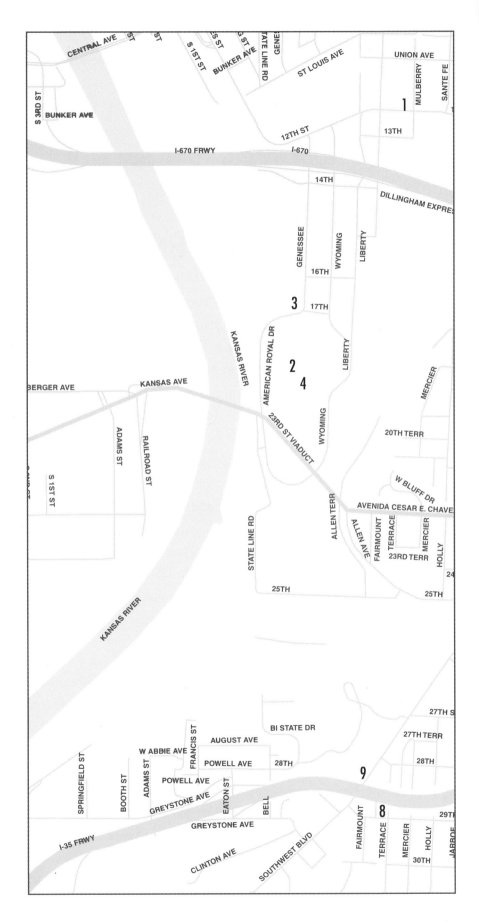

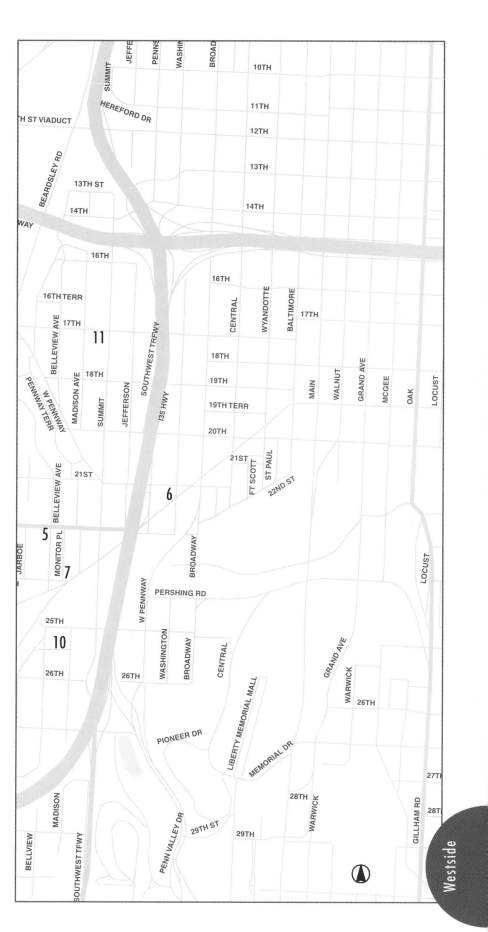

1 COMMERCIAL BUILDINGS, 1200-1418 W. 12TH STREET, 1879-1900. These two blocks of industrial/commercial buildings form one of the few surviving unaltered 19th century industrial streetscapes in Kansas City. Executed in red brick with stone detailing, the buildings display arched openings that pierce the wall and unify their three- and four-story façades. The 12th Street Viaduct, built in 1915, runs parallel to these buildings. It was the first double-deck concrete bridge in the United States and the first vehicular connection between the Central Business District and the West Bottoms.

2 R. CROSBY KEMPER SR. MEMORIAL ARENA, 1800 GENESSEE STREET, 1974, C.F. MURPHY ASSOCIATES, CHICAGO; RENOVATION AND EXPANSION, 1997, HNTB ARCHITECTS. Located on the former site of stockyards, the building features exterior steel trusses that support its massive structure. Renovations to this popular Kansas City arena included the addition of two escalators, restrooms, 2000 seats, a major new lobby and space for concession queues.

**3** KANSAS CITY LIVESTOCK EXCHANGE, 1600 GENESSEE STREET, 1910, WILDER & WIGHT. Constructed as the central headquarters of the Kansas City Stockyards, this building symbolizes Kansas City's success as a key trading center in the livestock industry and its instrumental role in the development of the West. The nine-story, E-plan, brick building overlooks the Kansas River and is surrounded by 207 acres once filled with stockyards and railroad tracks.

**4** BULL WALL, ROBERT MORRIS, 1800 GENESSEE STREET, AMERICAN ROYAL ARENA, 1992, STEEL, 16' x 47.5" x 120'. Childhood trips to the Kansas City Stockyards with his father inspired Morris to create this piece. The sculpture, comprised of two parallel walls, depicts 15 bulls stampeding and stomping up clouds of "dust," made by underground steam jets. A monument to the heritage of Kansas City and the tradition of the American Royal, this piece captures the essence and commotion of the Stockyards.

**5** GUADALUPE CENTER, 1015 W. 23RD STREET TRAFFICWAY, 1936, RANEY & CORMAN. Dorothy Gallagher, a Kansas City teacher, and other women provided prenatal and child health services to the large Mexican population in the Westside neighborhood. In 1919, the Center was established to provide immigrants with health care, social services and recreational activities. This Pueblo-style structure was commissioned by Gallagher's family and still serves area residents.

**6** COMMERCIAL BUILDING, 500 SOUTHWEST BOULEVARD, 1961, KIVETT AND MYERS AND MCCALLUM. Designed by innovative Kansas City architects, this unusual structure follows the example of the minimalist, modern style of Mies van der Rohe and other architects who developed the International style.

**7** FIRE STATION NO. 9, 901 SOUTHWEST BOULEVARD, 1887, ARCHITECT UNKNOWN. One of the oldest fire stations in the city, this brick structure has been renovated to house new businesses.

**8** KOCH SUPPLIES INC., 1411 W. 29TH STREET, 1978, SELIGSON ASSOCIATES, INC. This warehouse and equipment sales facility evokes the sparsely ornamented, streamlined modernism of the 1940s.

9 SOUTHWEST BOULEVARD PUMP STATION, 2800 BLOCK OF SOUTHWEST BOULEVARD, 1998, RAFAEL ARCHITECTS, INC. While most pump stations are visually uninteresting, people who live and work in this area articulated that they wanted this station to represent the cultural dynamic and vibrancy of their Westside neighborhood. In response to this desire, a unique design detail was integrated into the station façade. One corner of the building features illuminated glass block accents that give the appearance of "life" in the building. To avoid potential flooding problems, the pump station design incorporated a cast-in-place concrete flood wall set atop the existing foundation with subgrade chambers.

**10** SACRED HEART CATHOLIC CHURCH, 2544 MADISON AVENUE, 1896, ATTRIBUTED TO GUNN AND CURTISS. Father O'Dwyer, an immigrant from Limerick, Ireland, and his parishioners built this church and school. The stone construction, campanile and arched openings convey the Romanesque and Norman Revival styling. Other ornament includes a Celtic cross, stained glass windows and a sculpture of Christ.

**11** 17TH AND SUMMIT STREETS AREA. As early as the 1870s, this commercial and residential area served Irish and Mexican immigrants. Over the years, a large Mexican-American community developed in the neighborhood. In the 1980s and 90s, the area rebounded and now restaurants and businesses line the streets. Many area homes built in the late 1880s have also been restored.

# Old Northeast

NCOMPASSING THE LAND FROM TROOST AVENUE ON the west to Belmont Avenue on the east, and from the bluffs of the Missouri River south to Truman Road, the Old Northeast was an area of residential expansion for Kansas City, Missouri, in the late 1800s.

Around 1888, the bluffs were cleared and stately mansions constructed. Built on land donated by Nathan Scarritt, North Terrace Park connected with the city's new boulevards, and a meandering old cow path, Cliff Drive, became a landscaped road. The natural beauty of the location and the new system of boulevards attracted affluent families to the area. However, after 1920 descendants of the wealthy residents began to move to newly fashionable southern suburbs such as the Country Club Plaza, and smaller residences and apartments were built in the neighborhood. Many Italian immigrants settled in the Columbus Park area of the Old Northeast district, creating a "Little Italy."

Displaying a rich history of style and architecture, the Scarritt Point and Pendleton Heights historic districts and other individual properties have been well maintained and are listed on the National Register of Historic Places and the Kansas City Register of Historic Places.

Old Northeast

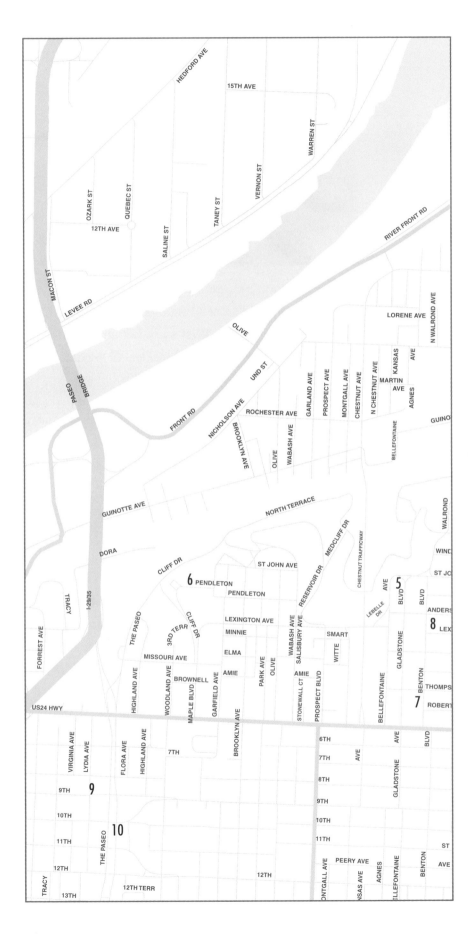

1 KANSAS CITY MUSEUM (R.A. LONG RESIDENCE), 3218 GLADSTONE BOULEVARD, 1911, HENRY F. HOIT. Built for a local lumber magnate and philanthropist, this house borders Kessler Park and is the most impressive Gladstone Boulevard mansion. An excellent example of beaux-arts-style architecture, the house features many fine woods, stained glass windows, and a double turned grand staircase that has inspired replicas in other, newer Kansas City buildings. In 1940, the Kansas City Museum opened in the mansion's Corinthian Hall. The museum houses a collection that focuses on regional history and artifacts.

## Parks & Boulevards

In the late 19th century, Kansas City leaders joined the "City Beautiful" movement; this plan called for the replacement of blighted urban areas with a series of parks and boulevards. In Kansas City, George Kessler, a young, talented urban planner, drew up a PARKS AND BOULEVARDS PLAN that included Gladstone Boulevard. Many prominent residents including R.A. Long encouraged and spurred the implementation of the plan in Kansas City.

**2** RESIDENCE, WILLIAM CHICK SCARRITT, 3240 NORLEDGE AVENUE, 1888, BURNHAM AND ROOT, CHICAGO. Overlooking Kessler Park, this Chateau-esque residence was built for William Scarritt, a prominent local lawyer, civic leader and advocate of the Parks and Boulevards system. The asymmetrical form, steeply pitched hip roof, prominent tower and masonry construction convey its architectural style. Constructed for $30,000, the home is distinguished by such details as leaded glass transoms, iron grillwork in the arched entrance and double-hung glass windows. It is significant for being the last known work in Kansas City designed by the distinguished American architectural firm, Burnham and Root.

**3** GLADSTONE BOULEVARD MANSIONS, 3500 (TOP) AND 3616
**4** (BOTTOM) GLADSTONE BOULEVARD. Generally constructed during the 1890s, elegant residences were built in Kansas City but only here do a sufficient number survive that the boulevard retains much of its original character. The area was home to many renowned Kansas Citians including R.A. Long and Reverend Nathan Scarritt and his decendents. At one time, so many judiciary officials occupied residences in the area that it was known as "Judges' Row."

Old Northeast

*67*

**5** PERISTYLE, ST. JOHN AVENUE AND GLADSTONE BOULEVARD, C.1896, JOHN VAN BRUNT. Built as part of the Parks and Boulevards system, this beaux-arts colonnade occupies a prominent position and exemplifies the grand scale of Kessler's plan for the city.

**6** RESIDENCE, PHILIP E. CHAPPELL, 1836 PENDLETON AVENUE, 1888, HARRY KEMP. Constructed during Kansas City's building boom in the 1880s, the three-story brick, limestone and wood shingle house served as a prototype for other houses in the area. A classic example of Queen Anne styling, this dwelling features an asymmetrical plan, multiple cladding materials, irregular roof lines and numerous porches. The cornice is made of pressed tin, ornamented with rosettes, fans and sawtooth cutwork. A two-story gabled porch accentuates the entrance.

**7** RESIDENCE, MILO E. LAWRENCE, 512 BENTON BOULEVARD, c.1888, ARCHITECT UNKNOWN. Built for the secretary and manager of the Standard Fire Insurance Company, this is one of the most exotic Queen Anne style houses in this area. A winged Assyrian figure of sculpted stone beautifully supports the second-story roof and towering gables grace the façade.

**8** ASSUMPTION CHURCH, 309 BENTON BOULEVARD, 1922-1927, CHESTER E. DEAN. It is recorded that the architect chose the Romanesque and Mission style elements for this church from two picture postcards. The interior was constructed without post supports, using a barrel vault suspended from steel beams. The exterior design elements include unusual brickwork, religious sculptures and crosses that top the entrance gable and two towers.

9 A. ZAHNER SHEET METAL COMPANY, 1400 E. NINTH STREET, 1983, SHAUGHNESSY FICKEL & SCOTT ARCHITECTS. A. Zahner Sheet Metal Company has been a member of the Kansas City business community for more than 100 years. The company's growth has demanded multiple additions to the physical plant. The latest expansion project included construction of a new shop and administrative offices. The building design blends the industrial character of corrugated sheet goods with simple detailing and craftsmanship.

10 THE PASEO PERGOLA, 1000 BLOCK OF THE PASEO, c.1899, JOHN VAN BRUNT. Another remarkable element of the Parks and Boulevards system, this beaux-arts structure consists of stepped Doric columns covered with beams. The semi-shaded arcade provides benches and an unobstructed view of The Paseo.

**11** CITY OF KANSAS CITY TRANSPORTATION OPERATIONS CENTER, 5310 MUNICIPAL AVENUE, 1988, CDFM$^2$ ARCHITECTURE. This redevelopment converted a trucking warehouse to a workplace for city employees. Designed by its architects as a town within a building, the structure houses offices, drafting, research and development areas, and dispatch, maintenance, meeting, break and locker rooms. Special interior elements include skylights, a streetscape circulation system, an indoor park with gazebo and landscaping, and a clock tower for orientation. The exterior features metal sheets that appear to be peeled away to reveal the new building.

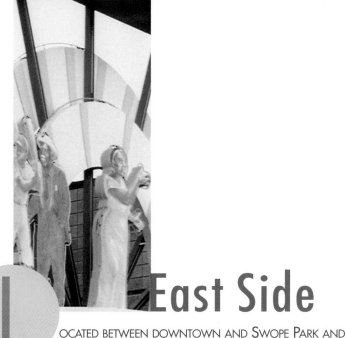

# East Side

OCATED BETWEEN DOWNTOWN AND SWOPE PARK AND from Troost Avenue to Interstate Highway 435, the east side of Kansas City, Missouri, is filled with residential and commercial areas significant for their multicultural history.

A farming community on the borders of Kansas City in the 1880s, this area grew as the city's cattle and transportation industries boomed. Buildings such as the Vine Street Workhouse and other public works and maintenance facilities were built around the beginning of the 20th century. Immigrant workers were among the first residents.

Another piece of the East Side's cultural history is found in the 18th and Vine District — the area where jazz and Kansas City's largest African-American community developed and flourished. During the 1880s and 1890s, many working and middle class black families moved into homes in this area.

As the black population grew in the area, 18th and Vine became the commercial and social center of the African-American community. Commercial, public and church buildings that housed black professionals and served the growing needs of area residents were built. The area reached its height as the center of African-American commerce and entertainment during the 1920s and 1930s. This period saw the growth of

East Side

theaters and jazz clubs such as the famous Gem Theatre and the Cherry Blossom Club. The Kansas City Monarchs, the Negro National League baseball team of Satchel Paige and Jackie Robinson, occupied offices there.

By the end of the 1920s, Kansas City was recognized nationally as a center for jazz musicians. Due to the varied economy, generous WPA work projects and the lax enforcement of Prohibition-era restrictions by "Boss Tom" Pendergast's administration, the Depression had less effect on Kansas City, and the area's 120 nightclubs and 40 dance halls continued to thrive. Many jazz musicians came to the area to find work and created Kansas City Jazz. Nightclubs such as the Jones Billiard Parlor on East 18th Street became hangouts for pace-setting musicians, including Walter Page, Duke Ellington, Bennie Moten, Count Basie, Andy Kirk and Charlie Parker.

With the end of the Pendergast era in 1939 and the beginning of World War II, Kansas City began to lose its status as a center of jazz. The civil rights and fair housing movements in the 1960s allowed the black community to integrate into other areas of the city and, as the population dispersed, many buildings were torn down. Today, the East Side includes numerous residential neighborhoods as well as industrial enclaves.

In the 1990s, community leaders launched an effort to refurbish the historic 18th and Vine District and the restored area is now a vibrant entertainment destination.

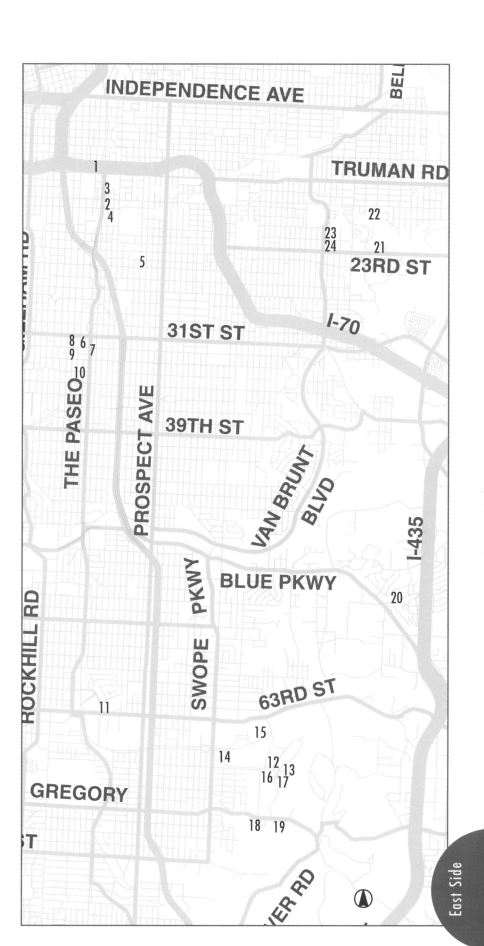

INDEPENDENCE AVE

TRUMAN RD

BELL

1

3
2
4

22

23
24

21

5

23RD ST

I-70

31ST ST

8 6
9 7

10

THE PASEO

PROSPECT AVE

39TH ST

VAN BRUNT BLVD

I-435

BLUE PKWY

20

ROCKHILL RD

SWOPE PKWY

11

63RD ST

15

14

12 13
16 17

GREGORY

18 19

VER RD

ST

1 St. Stephen Baptist Church, 1414 Truman Road, 1947, Ernest O. Brostrom. One of the principal churches in the black community for 50 years, this structure evokes the 1940s Moderne style. During his civil rights crusade, Dr. Martin Luther King Jr. spoke here.

2 Museums at 18th and Vine, 1616 E. 18th Street, 1997, Gould Evans Goodman Associates. Located on an entire block in this historic African-American cultural district, the 55,000 square-foot museum houses the Jazz and Negro Leagues Baseball museums, a visitors' center, an exhibit gallery and administrative offices. The complex incorporates two existing buildings with new construction. An arched entry forms a gateway into the transparent glass cube lobby. Outside a saxophone-shaped plaza and boldly patterned crosswalk decorate the exterior.

**3** *BIRD LIVES*, ROBERT GRAHAM, 17TH TERRACE AND VINE STREET, 1999, BRONZE, 17' x 64.5" x 69.75". A memorial to Kansas City, Kansas, native Charlie Parker, who began his legendary jazz career at 18th and Vine Streets. The Oppenheimer Fund commissioned this huge bronze bust to pay tribute to the African-American artists who lived and worked in the area. It also honors the birthplace of Kansas City Jazz.

# Historic 18th & Vine District

In the 1990s, city leaders began to campaign for the revitalization of the 18TH AND VINE DISTRICT, the residential and commercial area where the city's African-American population was centered in the early 20th century and where Kansas City Jazz was born. Soon after the effort began, the neighborhood underwent a vast redevelopment. Existing buildings were renovated and new buildings were constructed, creating museums and theaters, including the American Jazz Museum; the Negro Leagues Baseball Museum; the Horace M. Peterson III Visitor Center; The Blue Room, a jazz club in the museum that features local jazz artists; and the Gem Theatre, a restored venue for films and performances. The 18th and Vine Historic District celebrates and commemorates the social and economic development of the African-American community and Kansas City's jazz heritage.

East Side

**4** VINE STREET WORKHOUSE, 2001 VINE STREET, 1897, WALLACE LOVE AND JAMES OLIVER HOGG. Spurred by the hazardous environment of early Kansas City jails and the penal reform efforts, the city built this castellated limestone structure in order to improve conditions for prisoners. One of the few surviving late-19th century penal institutions in the area, the building originally featured a steam fan system, which provided fresh ventilation, and more spacious iron cells that reduced overcrowding and fire hazards.

**5** PARK AVENUE EVANGELICAL CHURCH, (NOW BOWERS MEMORIAL CHRISTIAN METHODIST CHURCH), 2456 PARK AVENUE, 1907, RUDOLF MARKGRAF. This early 20th century limestone church is a distinctive application of Mission Revival architecture to a religious building.

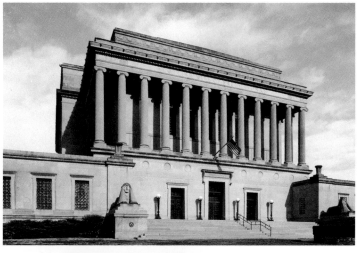

**6** Scottish Rite Temple, Linwood Boulevard and The Paseo, 1930, Keene and Simpson. This monumental beaux-arts civic structure has minimal ornament and a symmetrical façade that emphasize clean lines. Of particular interest are the pair of carved sphinxes that flank the grand staircase to the building's entrance.

**7** Stoplight, Linwood Boulevard and The Paseo, 1931, Edward Buehler Delk. Designed by the architect of the Country Club Plaza, this unusual cut-stone light fixture provides an eye-catching traffic solution.

8 CENTRAL PATROL POLICE STATION, 1200 E. LINWOOD BOULEVARD, 1994, GOULD EVANS ASSOCIATES. This 18,000 square-foot sculpted form occupies most of a city block. A circulation spine separates the structure into two triangular parts and continuous and individual windows punctuate the burnished masonry block.

9 *URBAN PALISADE*, JAY MARKEL, 1200 E. LINWOOD, 1994, IRON, 17' x 10' x 20'. Located on the site of the Central Patrol Police Station, this piece consists of green latticework that illustrates the structure of sculpture. Commissioned as part of the One-Percent-For-Art Program, it provides a colorful contrast to the geometric architecture of the station behind it.

**10** KENESETH ISRAEL-BETH SHALOM SYNAGOGUE (NOW CHRIST TEMPLE CHURCH), 3400 THE PASEO, 1927, GREENBAUM, HARDY AND SCHUMACHER. The twin terra cotta domes with elaborate displays of mosaic artwork distinguish this Byzantine-style structure. Other ornament includes doorway carvings of the Star of David.

**11** METRO POLICE PATROL DIVISION, 1880 E. 63RD STREET AT CITADEL STREET, 1977, PBNA ARCHITECTS. This municipal structure features terraced clerestories that allow natural light into the interior.

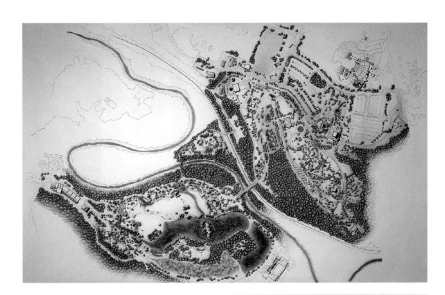

**12** KANSAS CITY ZOO MASTER PLAN AND DESIGN, 1991, BNIM ARCHITECTS. Utilizing new zoological design techniques, the architects increased the Zoo's area from 80 to 180 acres and divided the area into parcels which were developed to represent specific continents, such as Africa and Australia.

**13** *MERIDIAN; BONFIRE*, DEBORAH BUTTERFIELD, NEW ZOO PROJECT, 6700 ZOO DRIVE, 1995, BRONZE, 6'10" X 15' X 6'6". A One-Percent-For-Art Program commission, *Meridian* (standing horse) and *Bonfire* (reclining horse) appear to be made of curving vines and pieces of bleached driftwood. However, Butterfield's masterful pieces are actually cast bronze disguised to replicate their original organic forms.

**14** SHELTER HOUSE NO. 1, MEYER BOULEVARD AND SWOPE PARKWAY, 1905, ADRIANCE VAN BRUNT. The office of the Swope Park superintendent, this structure is an interpretation of Mission architecture. The fieldstone structure now houses the Swope Park Interpretive Center and administrative offices.

# S wope Park

Though originally an opponent of the Parks and Boulevards system, COL. THOMAS H. SWOPE, a Kansas City leader and philanthropist, purchased 1,350 acres of pasture and wooded land and in 1896 gave them to the city to create a huge public park. The park is one of the largest municipal parks in the country and its structures were built in various styles that reflect the natural setting. The Kansas City Zoo, the Starlight Theatre, two lakes, a swimming pool, park offices and the massive Swope Memorial are located here.

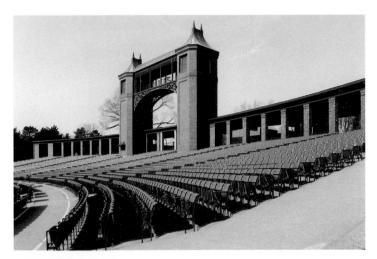

**15** STARLIGHT THEATRE, 4600 STARLIGHT DRIVE, 1951, EDWARD BUEHLER DELK; RENOVATION AND ADDITION, 2000, HNTB ARCHITECTS. Built by the architect who designed the Spanish-style Country Club Plaza, this open-air theater holds nearly 8,000 people and is surrounded by a curving portico supported by rectangular brick columns. A large arch, which holds the lighting booth, stands at the rear of the complex. In 2000, the theater added a new $10 million state-of-the-art stage house and two new towers with copper rooftops. The enclosed stage house is temperature-controlled and has a stage rigging system that allows for special effects and hanging scenery.

**16** AFRICAN PLAINS BARN, 6700 ZOO DRIVE, 1994, INTERNATIONAL ARCHITECTS ATELIER. Emulating the simple style of a barn, this structure was built to house African species ranging from giraffes to birds. A holding structure for New Zoo project exhibits, the barn is made of simple materials such as concrete masonry blocks, galvanized sheet metal and unfinished wood.

**17** DERAMUS EDUCATION PAVILION, 6700 ZOO DRIVE, 1995, BNIM ARCHITECTS. Built as part of the expansion and improvements to the Kansas City Zoo, this structure is the gateway to the Kingdom of Animals. The $16 million entry complex sets the mood of the zoo experience and includes an IMAX theater, banquet facilities, a restaurant, a gift shop, offices and storage space.

East Side

**18** LAKESIDE NATURE CENTER, 4701 E. GREGORY BOULEVARD, 1999, INTERNATIONAL ARCHITECTS ATELIER. This facility consists of 15,000 square feet of exhibition, classroom and support spaces, as well as animal rehabilitation areas. The natural site, including a flowing stream and a variety of exterior courtyard spaces, integrates with the designed structures.

**19** *THE RACE IS NOT ALWAYS TO THE SWIFT!*, KEN FERGUSON, LAKESIDE NATURE CENTER, 6700 ZOO DRIVE, 1999, BRONZE, 12" X 24" X 12". This bronze sculpture depicts the ubiquitous hare that has been a trademark of Ken Ferguson's pottery since 1985. Derived from the popular Aesop fable, *The Race is Not Always to the Swift!* cleverly matches Ferguson's hare with the Lakeside Nature Center's icon, a tortoise.

**20** METROPOLITAN AMBULANCE SERVICES TRUST HEADQUARTERS BUILDING, 6750 EASTWOOD TRAFFICWAY, 1997, SHAUGHNESSY FICKEL & SCOTT ARCHITECTS. Originally a big box retail store, this structure was renovated into a company headquarters. Transformed from a large rectangular box awash in a sea of surface parking space, the site now offers an interesting form that integrates three-dimensional volumes into existing structures.

**21** J.A. RODGERS ACADEMY OF LIBERAL ARTS AND SCIENCES, 6400 E. 23RD STREET, 1995, GOULD EVANS GOODMAN ASSOCIATES. Located on 22 acres of wooded land, the design of this magnet school takes advantage of the land's natural 130-foot vertical drop. The building emphasizes geometric shapes and consists of an overlapping three-story brick circle within a rectangular form.

**22** TRAILWOODS ENVIRONMENTAL SCIENCE MAGNET SCHOOL, 6201 E. 17TH STREET, 1995, MACKEY MITCHELL ZAHNER ASSOCIATES. Four separate yet connected buildings loosely assembled around the site compose this educational complex. Daylighting strategies, photovoltaic panels, a wind generator and the building materials enable the complex to harness natural energy. Most classrooms, as well as the learning center, greenhouse and cafeteria, are located on the south side of the building in order to take advantage of daylight. These south-facing rooms feature full-height glass curtain wall sections with exposed concrete floors for thermal storage.

**23** KANSAS CITY, MISSOURI, FIRE DEPARTMENT NO. 24, 22ND STREET AND HARDESTY AVENUE, 1980, SHAUGHNESSY FICKEL & SCOTT ARCHITECTS. The first Kansas City municipal building to utilize solar space heating, this fire station has poured concrete walls to provide elevation uniformity and to allow the solar panels to combine with rather than overwhelm the building's design.

**24** NEON SHAPES, WARREN ROSSER, 22ND STREET AND HARDESTY AVENUE, 1980, NEON TUBING, 15' x 1" x 15'. Installed on the exterior of the Kansas City, Missouri, Fire Station No. 24, the multicolored neon tubing forms a semaphore, a type of language/signal system used by the Navy, that spells out "K-C-F-D" (Kansas City Fire Department).

# Midtown

IDTOWN KANSAS CITY, MISSOURI, INCLUDES THE area from 31st Street south to 43rd Street and west from Troost Avenue to State Line Road.

During the early 1800s, pioneers such as John Calvin McCoy began to settle in the area. McCoy acquired and platted land in the western district of Missouri in 1833, and by 1846, "West Port" had become the stopping place for travelers on the Santa Fe and Oregon trails to stock up on goods and to stay overnight. In 1897, Westport was annexed to Kansas City, Missouri.

With the increase of industry in the downtown area, the improvement of roads and the advent of southern residential developments, many Kansas City, Missouri, residents began building and moving south in the late 19th and early 20th centuries. As a result, residential neighborhoods such as Hyde Park, Valentine, Union Hill and Janssen Place developed in the Midtown area and continue to boast fine examples of architecture. Recently, many structures in these neighborhoods have been renovated and neighborhood revitalization efforts are underway.

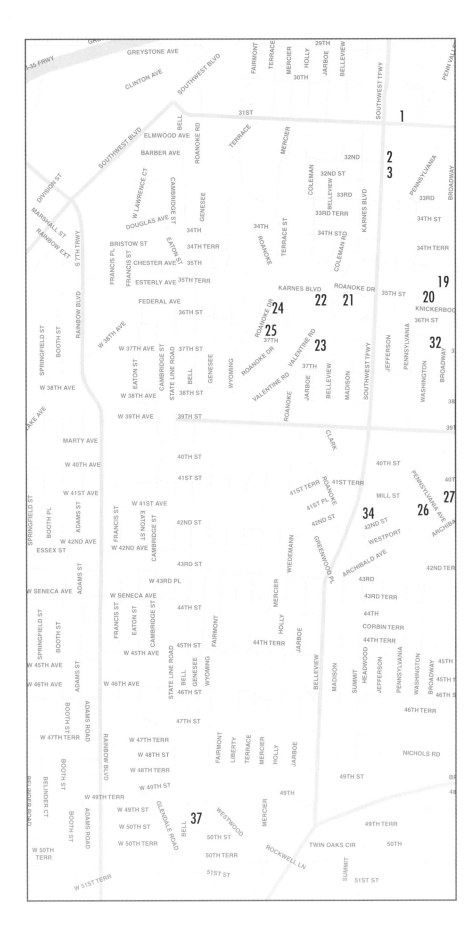

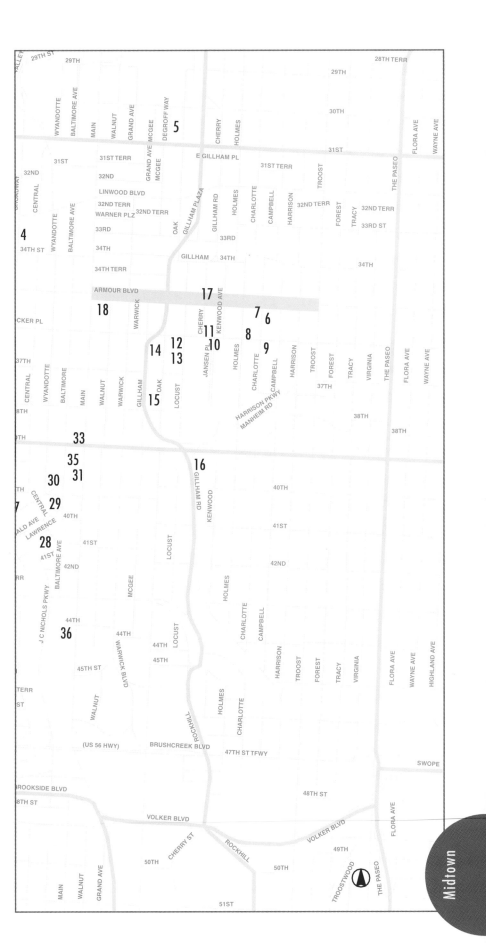

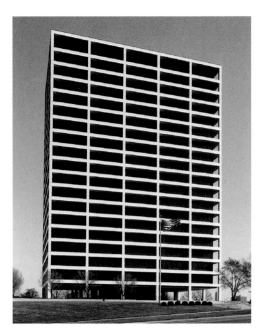

1 BMA BUILDING, 700 W. 31ST STREET, 1964, SKIDMORE, OWINGS & MERRILL. Located on one of the highest points in the city, on the hill overlooking Penn Valley Park, this building is notable as one of the first in Kansas City to have its support structure expressed on the exterior. Its exoskeleton is constructed of concrete with white Georgian marble cladding that forms a grid in front of the windows.

2 PENN VALLEY COMMUNITY COLLEGE, 3201 SOUTHWEST TRAFFICWAY, 1973, MARSHALL AND BROWN. This college complex was designed in a bold geometric style popular in the 1970s. Its planar walls are made up of brick expanses relieved only by the geometric openings of entrances and windows.

**3** FRANCIS CHILD DEVELOPMENT INSTITUTE, 3201 SOUTHWEST TRAFFICWAY, 1998, GOULD EVANS GOODMAN ASSOCIATES. This child care center responds to the planar architecture of Penn Valley Community College with curves and arcs to create a playful, contrasting environment. The addition's wall forms two arcs to layer and frame the space and the convex, projecting façade houses the Institute's office.

**4** OUR LADY OF PERPETUAL HELP REDEMPTORIST CATHOLIC CHURCH, 3333 BROADWAY, 1907-1912, WILDER AND WIGHT. Originally built to serve a small monastery in a quiet, rural area outside the city, this Gothic Revival-style church became one of the largest Catholic parishes in Kansas City. Three arched entrances, capped buttresses and a large circular stained glass window distinguished the main façade of this cruciform-plan limestone edifice.

Midtown

95

**5** RESIDENCES, 3000-3017 DEGROFF WAY, 1898-1899. William Rockhill Nelson, co-founder of *The Kansas City Star* and community activist and philanthropist, developed these blocks located in the Union Hill neighborhood. Built on alternate lots, these modest two-story houses make up an interesting, attractive and enduring city block. John Van Brunt, a distinguished Kansas City architect, lived at 3001 DeGroff Way.

# Hyde Park

Bounded by Armour and Harrison Boulevards, 39th Street and Gillham Road, the HYDE PARK HISTORIC DISTRICT is a turn-of-the-century neighborhood that was first platted in the 1880s and became one of the most popular southern suburbs at the beginning of the 19th century. Wealthy residents employed prominent architects such as Louis S. Curtiss, Frederick C. Gunn, John W. McKecknie and Clarence Shepard to build homes in a variety of architectural styles including Colonial Revival, Romanesque, Queen Anne, Shingle, Prairie School and Kansas City "Shirtwaist." Located on 7.8 acres within the historic district and designed by George E. Kessler, Hyde Park was a private park with a playground, tennis courts, and gardens; later, the park was converted into the Hyde Park Country Club and subsequently purchased by the Kansas City Parks Department. After World War II, many of the homes were converted into apartments; however, beginning in the 1970s many were restored to their original configuration and appearance.

**6** RESIDENCE, MARSHALL B. WRIGHT, 3535 CHARLOTTE STREET, 1898, ARCHITECT UNKNOWN. This three-story residence has a first-story, wrap-around porch and a second-story elevated side porch that is covered by a triangular gable.

7 RESIDENCE, 3530 CHARLOTTE STREET, 1912, SHEPARD, FARRAR AND WISER. This three-story Colonial Revival house features a grand portico with paired columns and a second-story balustrade. Sidelights and a transom frame the entrance. It was designed by one of Kansas City's prominent early 20th century architectural firms.

8 RESIDENCE, CHARLES E. GRANISS, 720 E. 36TH STREET, 1906, JOHN McKECKNIE. This house is distinguished by its unusual floor plan and elaborate exterior detail. The structure stands as a testament to the creativity of McKecknie, one of Kansas City's most beloved turn-of-the-century architects.

9 RESIDENCE, BENJAMIN H. BERKSHIRE, 3601 CHARLOTTE STREET, 1911, SHEPARD, FARRAR AND WISER. Built for a prominent lumberman, this expansive, vernacular residence is one of many built in the neighborhood for lumber barons.

10 JANSSEN PLACE HISTORIC DISTRICT, E. 36TH STREET AND JANSSEN PLACE, 1897-1917, GEORGE A. MATTHEWS. Planned by the railroad magnate Arthur Stilwell, this fashionable residential area was one of the first restricted neighborhoods in the city. After W.P. Patton, a local capitalist, bought the land and negotiated with the city to connect the neighborhood's main road with the Parks and Boulevards system, Janssen Place went through its busiest development period. Sixteen houses constructed between 1907-1917 display a variety of architectural styles. The area came to be known as "Lumberman's Row" because of the wealthy lumbermen who built houses there. The entrance to Janssen Place is marked by a neoclassical Revival-style gateway. Built in 1887, the gate is made of cut white Arkansas limestone and columnar pillars.

**11** RESIDENCE, ARTHUR MOSER, 600 E. 36TH STREET, 1892, ARCHITECT UNKNOWN. This was one of the six residences constructed by Janssen Place developer Arthur Stilwell. Built for a railroad executive, this Victorian Romanesque structure has an exterior façade of red limestone.

**12** RESIDENCE, 3608 LOCUST STREET, 1888; ADDITION, 1909, ARCHITECT(S) UNKNOWN. Jarvis Conklin, a 19th-century investment firm, built this Queen Anne-style house along with six others during the early development of the exclusive Hyde Park District.

Midtown

**13** RESIDENCE, 3632 LOCUST STREET, 1888, ARCHITECT UNKNOWN. Another house built by the investment firm of Jarvis Conklin, this form combines Queen Anne and Shingle styles. Notable residents of this house included H.M. Beardsley, a mayor of Kansas City, and Herbert Hadley, a governor of Missouri.

**14** RESIDENCE, 3605 GILLHAM ROAD, 1888, ARCHITECT UNKNOWN. The Historic Kansas City Foundation saved this unusual Victorian brick and stone structure from demolition in 1976. It was then sold to private owners and is one of the many carefully restored and maintained houses in the historic Hyde Park District.

**15** HYDE PARK TOWNHOMES, 3735-3747 GILLHAM ROAD, 1985, PBNI ARCHITECTS. Located on the edge of the Hyde Park neighborhood, these six townhomes use contemporary design to express traditional residential forms.

**16** PARKS AND RECREATION DISTRICT 2 BUILDING, 39TH STREET AND GILLHAM ROAD, 1904, ADRIANCE VAN BRUNT & CO. Built during a period of frenzied construction in the Hyde Park area and originally used as the Parks and Recreation stables, this office building uses a mixture of native limestone and brick trim.

Midtown

**17** ARMOUR BOULEVARD, WALNUT STREET TO TROOST AVENUE. At the turn of the century, this wide street was lined with elm trees and elegant limestone residences built by prominent local architects. Planned as an affluent residential quarter and included in the Parks and Boulevards system, this boulevard was made fashionable when Kirkland B. Armour, a local meat-packing industry baron, built a mansion in 1893 at the corner of Armour and Warwick Boulevards. As the city grew, many of the single-family residences along the Boulevard were replaced by apartments and hotels between the 1910s and 1930s. Recently, the area has been a focus of redevelopment and many structures have been restored.

**18** RESIDENCE, 3534 WALNUT STREET, 1890, ARCHITECT UNKNOWN. Built for William Baker Knight, a nationally recognized civil engineer who designed and constructed several Kansas City cable railroad lines, this house combines 19th century Revival styles. The façade of this half-timbered house features stone, timber and high arches on two sides of the residence.

**19** KANSAS CITY LIFE INSURANCE BUILDING, 3520 BROADWAY, 1924, WIGHT AND WIGHT. Designed by a Kansas City architectural firm noted for its use of classical motifs, this building is an excellent example of beaux-arts architecture.

**20** KNICKERBOCKER APARTMENTS, KNICKERBOCKER PLACE, 1910, LEON MIDDAUGH. These colonnade-style buildings contain a 56-unit residential complex at a once-fashionable Kansas City address. Initially located on a private street, the apartments had such famous residents as Lucy Wornall and Jean Harlow. Though part of the complex was demolished, the remaining three-story brick buildings provide large front porches for each unit.

Midtown

**21** RESIDENCE, SONDERN/ADLER, 3600 BELLEVIEW
AVENUE, 1940; ADDITION, 1950; FRANK LLOYD
WRIGHT. This home was designed for Clarence
Sondern by the internationally renowned architect
in his Usonian style. Ten years later, Wright added a
large living room to the T-shaped plan a quarter
story below the original structure for a new owner.

**22** THOMAS HART BENTON HOME, STUDIO AND VISITORS CENTER, 3616 BELLEVIEW AVENUE, 1904, GEORGE MATTHEWS; RESTORATION, 1993, PGAV ARCHITECTS. Thomas Hart Benton, one of America's foremost 20th century artists, lived and worked for more than 40 years in these structures. The two-and-one-half story home and the two-story carriage house are Victorian in style and are covered with ashlar limestone. The home served as a residence and Benton's gallery; the carriage house was Benton's studio where guests such as Harry S. Truman and Carl Sandberg visited Benton and his wife, Ruth. In 1993, the house and studio were renovated and preserved to retain the house's style at the time of Benton's death in 1975. The garage was converted into a Visitor's Center that features an enlarged copy of one of Benton's famed murals.

**23** RESIDENCE, ALBERT J. YANDA, 1102 VALENTINE ROAD, 1966, ALBERT J. YANDA. Acting as the architect, builder and owner, Albert Yanda built this detached structure as a labor of love. Located in an established neighborhood of early 20th century residences, this home's most striking design features are the structural steel supports, stilts and triangular steel panels.

**24** RESIDENCE, NORMAN TROMANHAUSER, 3603 W. ROANOKE DRIVE, 1915, LOUIS S. CURTISS. Designed for his friends by one of Kansas City's treasured architects, the structure combines the low, horizontal lines of the Prairie School and the banded openings of Arts and Crafts, resulting in Curtiss' unique style. Geometric wood screens, small gabled peaks and a red tile roof give the small dwelling a distinctive, Oriental flair.

**25** RESIDENCE, LUSTRON HOUSE, 3605 ROANOKE ROAD, MORRIS H. BECKMAN. Lustron houses were unique all-steel dwellings built between 1948 and 1950. The Lustron Corporation adapted automotive assembly line techniques to residential construction in an effort to create a pre-fabricated house that would address the post-World War II housing shortage. Approximately 2,500 Lustrons were built nationwide before the federal government foreclosed on the company's outstanding loans. Available in two- and three-bedroom models, these dwellings resembled the design of typical wood frame post-war dwellings. However, their steel frames clad on the interior and exterior with porcelain enamel-coated steel panels distinguished Lustrons from more traditional contemporary residential construction. Other distinctive features included radiant heating and numerous built-ins.

# Westport

In 1833, John Calvin McCoy opened the first trading post on land located on the Santa Fe and Oregon trail route and near the Missouri riverfront. He platted "West Port," encouraged the transportation of commercial goods via the river and began outfitting travelers. Due to its prime location, by 1846 McCoy's business and town thrived and became one of the busiest sections of the growing area. By the end of the century, Kansas City had expanded to meet the borders of WESTPORT, and in 1897 the town was annexed. Westport retains many of its historic structures and is a vital residential, commercial and entertainment district.

**26** ALBERT G. BOONE STORE, 500 WESTPORT ROAD, 1851; ADDITIONS, 1880-1882, 1894-1904; ARCHITECT(S) UNKNOWN. Kansas City's oldest surviving commercial building, this store was the trading post operated by Daniel Boone's grandson to outfit travelers along the Santa Fe and Oregon trails. Several additions and many years later, the structure houses the locally famous bar, *Kelly's*.

**27** WESTPORT SQUARE, WESTPORT ROAD BETWEEN BROADWAY AND PENNSYLVANIA AVENUES, RENOVATION, 1972-1978. Since 1833, this area has been a busy commercial hub. The late-19th century brick structures were renovated in the 1970s and house a variety of shops, restaurants and businesses. The Square is the center of the Westport entertainment district.

Midtown

**28** RESIDENCE, REV. NATHAN SCARRITT, 4038 CENTRAL STREET, C.1847; RENOVATION, 1970; ARCHITECT(S) UNKNOWN. Built by Joseph Boggs and sold to Rev. Scarritt in the 1850s, this is a typical mid-19th century frame house and is noted as one of the oldest structures in Westport. An important Westport figure, Rev. Scarritt, who had taught at the Shawnee Mission Indian Training School, helped build and administer Westport High School.

**29** RESIDENCE, JOHN HARRIS, 4000 BALTIMORE, C.1855; ADDITION, C.1870; ARCHITECT(S) UNKNOWN. Thought to be the oldest surviving brick home in Kansas City, this antebellum Greek revival residence was built by Colonel John Harris. Harris, a pioneer himself, owned the  Harris House, Westport's most popular hotel among Santa Fe and Oregon Trail travelers. The structure was later purchased by William Rockhill Nelson, co-founder of *The Kansas City Star,* and was in danger of being demolished. However, in 1922, it was moved from its original location on Westport Road to its current location on Baltimore. It now houses the Westport Museum and the headquarters of the Westport Historical Society.

**30** Westport Public Library, 118 Westport Road, 1889, Grant B. Middaugh; renovation, 1998, Mackey Mitchell Zahner Architects. Originally the Allen Library, this structure was built in 1889 as a result of Judge A.M. Allen's discovery of $7,500 in surplus tax funds left over from the construction of a horse railroad from Kansas City to Westport. The twin-towered building is one of Westport's oldest structures and continues to serve its many patrons. Its distinctive design includes slate shingles and two-story conical bays. In 1998, the library was renovated and modern conveniences such as elevators were added.

**31** Drug store, 3948 Main Street, 1938, Clarence Kivett. An early design of Clarence Kivett, a Kansas City architectural legend, the structure emulates the architecture at the Chicago World's Fair in 1933. Originally built for Katz Drug Company, a local drug store chain, the building has been in continual use by various drug stores.

**32** Uptown Theater, 3700 Broadway, 1927, John Eberson, New York City, and Robert Gornall; addition and renovation, 1999, Gould Evans Goodman Associates. This former movie palace is significant for its lighted dome, its huge over-hanging marquee and its interior Italian garden motif. Purchased by Universal Pictures and later 20th Century Fox, it remained a popular movie theater until 1972. In 1999, the building's renovation included a three-story addition. The upgraded theater now serves as a popular concert venue.

**33** Terra Cotta Buildings, 38th to 40th Streets on Main Street. After Main Street — the first "South Side" north-south trafficway — was completed in 1926, these commercial buildings were built to serve the district's growing southern suburban residential population. Designed by prestigious architects, including Thomas Wight, John McKecknie, Clarence Kivett and Shepard, Farrar and Wiser, the structures housed shops, offices, entertainment establishments and movie palaces. They include the best examples of polychrome Art Deco terra cotta in the city. At the *Jack O'Lantern Ballroom*, located at 3936 Main Street, Joan Crawford won the Charleston contest that launched her movie career.

**34** WESTPORT HOUSE, 4020 MILL STREET, 1983, ABEND SINGLETON ASSOCIATES. This housing development's wedge-shaped apartments provide a space-saving foyer at each floor. The elimination of one wedge allows natural light to fill the building's center. Building ornament includes a stained glass butterfly. Varied brick surface textures provide viewers with visual surprises from every angle.

**35** CALVARY BAPTIST CHURCH, 3921 BALTIMORE AVENUE, 1890, WILLIS W. POLK; ADDITIONS, 1940, 1949, 1965, ARCHITECT(S) UNKNOWN. This native stone Romanesque Revival-style building was designed by a member of the congregation. The large dome required no center posts or supports and the interior arches are made of walnut beams. The façade is embellished by a fanlight window.

**36** H&R BLOCK HEADQUARTERS, 4400 MAIN STREET, 1980, MARSHALL AND BROWN; ADDITION, 1994, BNIM ARCHITECTS. Located at this site since 1951, H&R Block has steadily expanded its facilities. In 1994, as part of the company's commitment to the Main Street Corridor, the company elected to renovate and expand rather than move. The result was an upgrade of the existing three-story structure and construction of a new four-story, 93,000 square-foot office building and a 45,200 square-foot pre-cast concrete garage.

**37** RESIDENCE, 4955 BELL STREET, 1998, GASTINGER WALKER HARDEN. This 2,200 square-foot townhouse incorporates current technology to minimize maintenance and energy consumption. Private porches and varying sizes of rectangular and circular windows grace the exterior.

# Brush Creek & Country Club

**A**DJACENT TO MIDTOWN AND BOUNDED BY TROOST Avenue, 63rd Street and State Line Road, the Brush Creek and Country Club district in Kansas City, Missouri, comprises a vast area of residential, cultural, educational and commercial centers.

Used as battle grounds by soldiers during the Civil War and traversed by pioneers heading west on the Santa Fe and Oregon trails, this land was pasture with marshes, dirt roads and farms until the turn of the 20th century.

In 1908, with great vision and at considerable risk, Jesse Clyde Nichols, a real estate investor and developer, purchased 4,000 acres there and began planning a new residential and commercial district, the Country Club area. For years, Kansas City had been expanding southward and Nichols' innovative development of the residential neighborhoods with nearby commercial centers proved to be wise. Affluent families began building high quality homes that featured Colonial, Georgian, Tudor and Italianate styles. Nichols' Country Club Plaza, designed by Edward Buehler Delk in a Spanish style, was the first planned business and shopping complex of its kind in the country.

The district is dotted with museums, churches, residential neighborhoods, boulevards, fountains and colleges. It remains one of Kansas City's most popular areas in which to live, work and shop.

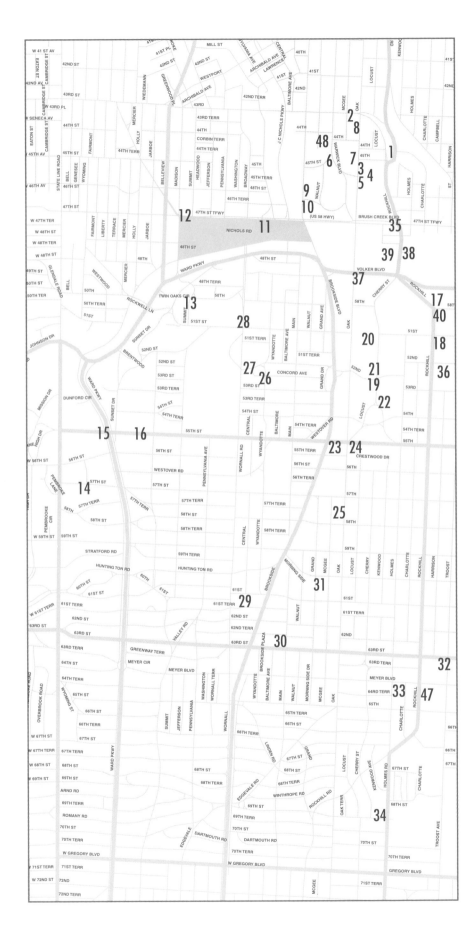

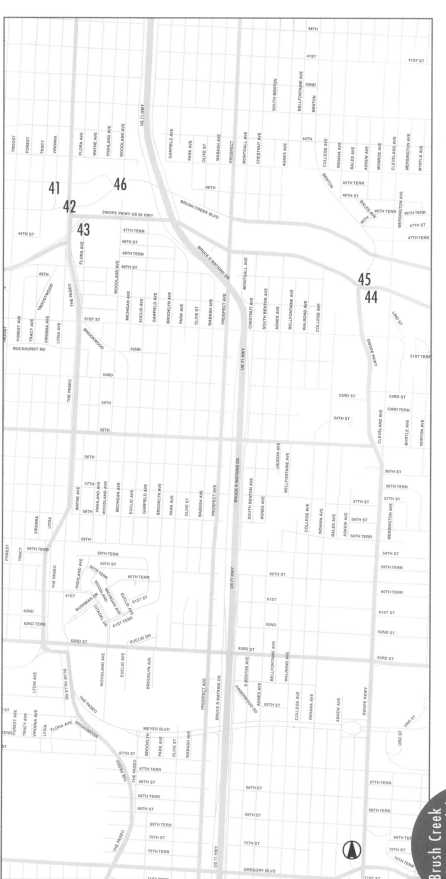

41
46
42
43
45
44

**1** ROCKHILL TOWNHOUSES, W. GILLHAM ROAD FROM 43RD TO 45TH STREETS, 1962, PETER KELETI & ASSOCIATES. Surrounded by a stone wall that extends throughout the Rockhill neighborhood, these timber and native limestone townhouses are very similar in style and construction.

**2** APARTMENTS, EAST 43RD, OAK AND McGEE STREETS, 1922, ARCHITECT UNKNOWN. William A. Rule, the original owner of Mineral Hall, lived in a 20-room stone mansion on this property. The need for more residential housing resulted in the demolition of the mansion and the construction of these classically designed apartments that feature three-story Corinthian columns, front porches with railings of turned balusters and a projecting cornice. The stone wall that originally surrounded Rule's estate still stands on the property.

**3** NELSON-ATKINS MUSEUM OF ART, 4525 OAK STREET, 1930-33, WIGHT AND WIGHT.
Located on the site of William Rockhill Nelson's residence, Oak Hall, this museum
was built after his death through a massive bequest and the contributions of art
enthusiast, Mary Atkins. The neoclassical structure is sheathed in limestone relief
panels carved by Charles Keck. This Kansas City landmark houses one of the
world's significant art collections and is internationally known for its outstanding
collections of Asian art and modern sculpture.

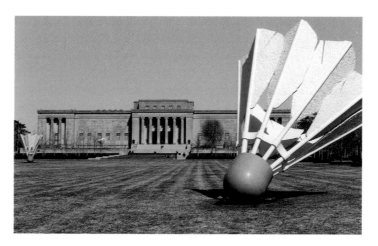

**4** *SHUTTLECOCKS*, 4525 OAK STREET, 1994, CLAES
OLDENBURG AND COOSJE VAN BRUGGEN, ALUMINUM AND
FIBERGLASS, EACH APPROXIMATELY 18.75' X 17.5' X 16'.
Acquired through the Sosland Family in 1994, Claes
Oldenburg's and Coosje van Bruggen's playful
*Shuttlecocks* are perhaps the most controversial
additions to the Kansas City Sculpture Park and have
become a recognized symbol of Kansas City. The four
aluminum and fiberglass sculptures depict giant
white-feathered badminton "birds," one on the north
side and three on the south side of the museum. The
south and north lawns of the museum represent a
badminton court and the museum building stands tall
as the symbolic badminton net.

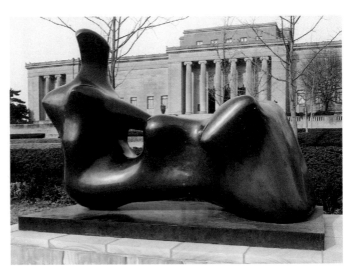

**5** Kansas City Sculpture Park, Nelson-Atkins Museum of Art, 47th and Oak Streets and Rockhill Road, 1989, Kiley & Robertson. One of the finest collections of modern sculpture in the world, the Kansas City Sculpture Park began in 1986 when the Hall Family Foundation acquired a group of Henry Moore bronze sculptures. The Nelson-Atkins Museum of Art and the Kansas City Board of Parks and Recreation Commissioners, the owners of the 44 acres of public land surrounding the Museum, and the Hall Family Foundation worked together to create the Henry Moore Sculpture Garden in 1989. The collection soon began to grow — in 1991 masterpieces by Brancusi, Ernst, and Giacometti were acquired and works by Elie Nadelman, Ossip Zadkine, and Donald Judd were given to the museum by collectors. The Modern Sculpture Initiative in 1992 emphasized a focus on acquiring modern sculpture. The 17-acre park was renamed the Kansas City Sculpture Park in 1999. As a result, the museum's modern sculpture collection has grown significantly over the years. This is the largest collection of Henry Moore's bronze sculptures outside Great Britain. These 14 abstract pieces include *Reclining Figure: Hand, Large Interior Form, Upright Motive No. 9, Sheep Piece* and *Three Way Piece No. 1: Points*, and represent the female figure as the embodiment of nature.

6 VANDERSLICE HALL, KANSAS CITY ART INSTITUTE, 4415 WARWICK BOULEVARD, 1896, VAN BRUNT AND HOWE. The college was created in 1885, when a group interested in art formed a "sketch club." Noted as one of the top art schools in the nation, the Art Institute's alumni include Walt Disney, Robert Morris and Richard Notkin. In the 1920s, board member Howard Vanderslice purchased the August R. Meyer residence to serve as the school's new home. Renamed Vanderslice Hall, it now houses the administration office. Other buildings on the campus have been designed by David Runnels and Marshall and Brown. Below is the East Building, 1971, by Marshall and Brown.

7 EAST GATE PIECE, DALE ELDRED, KANSAS CITY ART INSTITUTE, 4415 WARWICK BOULEVARD, 1966, WOOD AND STEEL, EACH PANEL APPROXIMATELY 14' x 15" x 7'. This abstract, geometric sculpture was one of the many gifts that Dale Eldred, an internationally renowned artist and sculpture chair of the Kansas City Art Institute for more than thirty years, contributed to the community.

**8** MINERAL HALL, KANSAS CITY ART INSTITUTE, 4340 OAK STREET, 1904, LOUIS S. CURTISS. Another treasure designed by one of Kansas City's most popular architects, Mineral Hall is a mixture of Art Nouveau and neoclassical elements. Constructed but never lived in by William A. Rule, director of the Kansas City Life Insurance Company, the magnificent turn-of-the-century house was first occupied by Roland E. Bruner, a mining tycoon. The arched main entrance is a distinctive Art Nouveau design that incorporates imported mosaic and leaded glass. Bruner kept his 10,000-piece collection of mineral specimens in the north addition. Today, the house holds the school's admissions department.

**9** Community Christian Church, 4601 Main Street, 1940, Frank Lloyd Wright. After losing its original building in a fire, the Linwood Christian Church commissioned Wright to build this "contemporary" structure because of his record for designing safe buildings. The hexagon building Wright designed had a steel frame coated with sprayed concrete. From the beginning, Wright had a difficult time progressing on the project. The first obstacle occurred when city codes inspectors refused to allow the crushed rock foundation he proposed. Wright insisted that a standard concrete foundation would cause the building to crack and later, it did. Frustrated by local bureaucracy, Wright walked away from the project. In 1940, architect Edward Buehler Delk completed the church.

**10** Light Steeple, Frank Lloyd Wright, 4601 Main Street, designed 1940; completed 1994. Not satisfied with traditional church steeples, Wright designed these four 300-pound lights to crisscross and form a steeple made of light. Due to budgeting limitations, wartime blackouts and lack of requisite technology, the steeple was left unfinished. In the 1990s, however, renowned Kansas City artist and sculptor Dale Eldred and his wife, Roberta, began to experiment with lights that would complete Wright's vision. When Eldred tragically perished in an accident, the local art community was determined to finish the project and in 1994, the 4,500-watt lamps were switched on. Now, they shine brilliantly from 7 to 10 p.m. on Fridays, Saturdays, holy days and during the Christmas season.

**11** COUNTRY CLUB PLAZA, BEGUN 1922, EDWARD BUEHLER DELK, 1922-25; EDWARD TANNER, 1925-74. The Country Club Plaza is one of the nation's earliest master-planned shopping districts. Inspired by his European travels, developer Jesse Clyde Nichols enlisted Edward Buehler Delk to design a shopping complex that featured Spanish architecture and decoration. After visiting Seville, Spain, Delk proposed the use of Spanish and Mexican motifs including stucco and tile work and Nichols declared it the official Country Club style. The district still retains Spanish-style towers, and various commercial buildings incorporate decorative tile, ironwork, painted stucco and terra cotta ornamentation.

# ountry Club Plaza & Residential District

In 1908, Jesse Clyde Nichols, developer and realtor, announced that he intended to build a residential area south of the Central Business District. The plans called for integrated topography. At that time, the area now called the COUNTRY CLUB PLAZA & RESIDENTIAL DISTRICT was surrounded by marshes and Main Street was a narrow country lane with no utilities or pavement. The city was moving rapidly southward and Nichols envisioned a total environment that provided shops, schools and churches for quality residences. Today, the Country Club area is perhaps the most popular residential and shopping district in Kansas City. It plays host to the annual Christmas lighting ceremony, fairs and parades, and features beautiful architecture.

**12** PLAZA CENTER BUILDING, 800 W. 47TH STREET, 1963, SKIDMORE, OWINGS & MERRILL, CHICAGO. Similar to the BMA Building, this is an example of an expressed structural frame, this time with pre-cast concrete elements which project beyond the glass walls on all sides, adding visual depth to the design.

**13** RESIDENCES, ROCKWELL AND HOOK, 4950 SUMMIT STREET, 1922; AND 5011 SUNSET DRIVE, 1928; MARY ROCKWELL HOOK. One of Kansas City's early successful female architects, Hook built three houses in this area for members of her family. She was well-educated, widely traveled and enjoyed incorporating various styles, especially French and Italian, in each structure that she designed. The open courtyards that surround the stone structures reflect her admiration for Italian villas and successfully capture the beauty of the sloping site.

**14** RESIDENCE, 1231 W. 57TH STREET, 1972, HUGH NEWELL JACOBSEN. The contemporary styling of this structure includes several rectangular sections connected by a series of corridors.

**15** RESIDENCE, BERNARD CORRIGAN, 1200 W. 55TH STREET, 1913, LOUIS S. CURTISS. Located in the Sunset Hill section of the Country Club Plaza, this residence is known as Louis Curtiss' masterpiece. The form, low-hipped with banded windows, alludes to the Prairie School style. However, Curtiss' typically eclectic design also includes Art Nouveau masonry relief, Arts and Crafts ornament and stained glass, and a Mediterranean tile roof.

**16** RESIDENCE, SETH E. WARD, 1032 W. 55TH STREET, c.1871, ASA BEEBE CROSS. Located on the site of Civil War fighting, this is one of the few surviving Greek Revival-style houses in the city. The 212-acre area was purchased from William Bent, a noted pioneer in the western frontier, by Seth Ward, a Santa Fe trader who earned his fortune negotiating with Native Americans and travelers. While the form and massing of the house are Greek Revival, the porch elements reflect early Victorian styling popular in the years following the Civil War. The exterior of this farmhouse is clad with brick produced from local materials, and Italianate additions such as the veranda modify the original design.

**17** THE STOWERS INSTITUTE FOR MEDICAL RESEARCH, 5007 ROCKHILL ROAD, 2000, PGAV ARCHITECTS. James Stowers and his wife, Virginia, commissioned this structure to house a world-class research center that would attract the world's top scientists. This center is located on the grounds of the old Menorah Hospital. Three existing hospital buildings were renovated and one new 265,000 square-foot building was constructed. The façade of each structure was covered with buff-colored concrete.

# University of Missouri–Kansas City

Now comprising more than 85 acres, the school began in 1929 as Kansas City University when William Volker, local philanthropist and businessman, deeded land to the college's board. Volker also issued the funds to purchase the Walter S. Dickey mansion, used for classrooms, a library, a cafeteria and administrative offices. University buildings are characterized by native stone exteriors and timber decoration. Since becoming the University of Missouri–Kansas City in 1963, the school has continued to expand due to increasing enrollment.

**18** RESIDENCE, WALTER S. DICKEY, 5100 ROCKHILL ROAD, 1912, ROGER GILMAN. A gift to the school from William Volker, this Renaissance-style stone mansion was built for Walter Dickey, a manufacturer and newspaper publisher, at the cost of $100,000. A grand hall and staircase off the north terrace emphasize the large scale of the house. Today it houses the university administration offices.

**19** RESIDENCE, U.S. EPPERSON, 5200 CHERRY STREET, 1927, HORRACE LAPIERRE. This Tudor manor-style mansion was designed with the help of the owner. Key stylistic elements include brick and stone cladding, a castellated tower and parapet walls, simulated half-timbering and diamond-paned leaded glass windows. The house was later purchased by the University and converted into classrooms. It now houses the University of Missouri–Kansas City Architectural Studies office that operates in conjunction with Kansas State University.

**20** RESIDENCE, EDWIN W. SHIELDS, 5110 CHERRY STREET, 1909, WILDER AND WIGHT; RESTORATION AND ADDITION, 1988, SOLOMON CLAYBAUGH YOUNG AND ARCHITECTURAL RESOURCES, CAMBRIDGE, MASS. Named "The Oakland" by its original owner, E.W. Shields, a grain company president, it has since served as a private preparatory school, a seminary and a business school. In 1988, a 43,000 square-foot, U-shaped addition was constructed on the west side of the original structure.

**21** LINDA HALL LIBRARY, 5109 CHERRY STREET; MAIN BUILDING, 1956; ANNEX, 1964; EDWARD W. TANNER AND ASSOCIATES. Located on the property of Herbert F. Hall and funded by a $6 million donation in memory of his wife, this library is one of the largest privately endowed scientific and technical libraries in the world.

**22** RESIDENCE, 5305 CHERRY STREET, 1966, BRUCE GOFF. Built in a well-established neighborhood, this whimsical residence utilizes a circular, geometric design plan. It is popularly called the "fish house" and the "tee pee house" because of its unusual design elements.

**23** CRESTWOOD NEIGHBORHOOD, c.1919. One of J.C. Nichols' earliest residential developments, the street planning utilized the area's rolling topography. Wooded with indigenous maple and oak trees, the neighborhood features a shared park and many noteworthy homes, designed in various styles including Tudor and Colonial Revival.

**24** CRESTWOOD SHOPS, 55TH STREET BETWEEN OAK STREET AND BROOKSIDE DRIVE, 1922, EDWARD TANNER. Built to service the adjacent Crestwood Neighborhood, these red brick Colonial Revival-style shops were once served by streetcar. The shops were part of the J.C. Nichols Company's efforts to develop a neighborhood commercial center in conjunction with a residential area.

**25** BUNGALOWS, OAK STREET FROM 55TH TO 63RD STREETS. This area provides many examples of the Bungalow-style residences common in Kansas City. Typical bungalows have steeply pitched roofs and front porches, often covering the full width of the façade. During the 1930s housing shortages, these houses provided plenty of urban housing without compromising space and appearance.

Brush Creek & Country Club

131

**26** RESIDENCE, JOHN J. WOLCOTT, 5225 WYANDOTTE STREET, 1915, SHEPHARD, FARRAR AND WISER. This residence imitates the Prairie School style that Frank Lloyd Wright developed at the turn of the 20th century. The shallow-hipped roof with wide, overhanging eaves and banded windows are identifying elements of this style.

**27** RESIDENCE, WILLIAM H. COLLINS, 232 W. 52ND STREET, 1924, EDGAR C. FARIS. Known as the "Villa del Sol," this elegant Mediterranean-style mansion is distinguished by its parapeted dormer. The tile roof, bracketed window hoods, a second-story balcony, and a triple-arched, recessed entrance are defining architectural elements.

**28** THE WALNUTS, 5049 WORNALL ROAD, 1930, BOILLOT AND LAUCK. This has been a fashionable address since Mrs. Jacob Loose, who donated the land for Loose Park, chose to relocate here after her husband died. These Jacobean-style buildings were built with limited Tudor architectural references, such as the exterior concrete pilasters, projecting bays and stone trim. The apartment units feature spacious living quarters, high-quality service and modern conveniences.

**29** JOHN B. WORNALL HOUSE, 146 W. 61ST TERRACE, 1858, ARCHITECT UNKNOWN. This Greek Revival-style, antebellum farmhouse is owned and maintained by the Jackson County Historical Society. Built of red brick with wood trim, it is distinguished by its two-story pedimented front porch and recessed second-story balcony. The house was originally part of an 1,110-acre plantation and during the Civil War it served as a Union headquarters.

**30** COUNTRY CLUB POLICE AND FIRE STATION, 22 W. 63RD STREET, 1917, FREDERICK H. MICHAELIS. Built by the J.C. Nichols Company, this structure was designed to complement the Company's nearby residential and commercial development by using similar materials and architectural styling.

**31** RESIDENCE, DR. SAMUEL AYRES, 6036 MCGEE STREET, 1915, SELBY KURFISS. This classic Arts and Crafts bungalow features a full-width front porch, stone body and roof dormers. The curved edges of the roof suggests the thatch roofs of English cottages.

**32** MERCANTILE BANK, 6300 TROOST AVENUE, DATE AND ARCHITECT UNKNOWN; RENOVATION, 1975, ABEND SINGLETON ASSOCIATES. The renovation of this 1920s brick structure occurred during the mid-1970s and resulted in an interesting juxtaposition of the two periods' architectural styles.

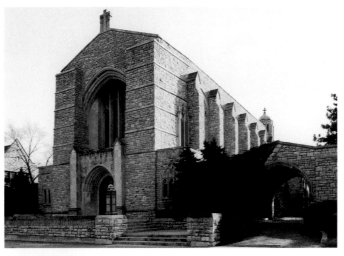

**33** St. Peter's Parish, 6415 Holmes Street, 1946, Caroll and Dean Architects; addition, 1999, Gould Evans Goodman Associates. Like many churches in the area, this large structure is built of native limestone. The English Gothic-style church and school sit side by side and form a cloistered garden.

**34** Temple B'nai Jehudah, 712 E. 69th Street, 1958; addition, 1969, Kivett and Myers. A prominent architectural firm designed the original structure and, 10 years later, added a tentlike sanctuary supported by an 83-foot concrete center stabilizing pole. LaFarge windows, first located in the Linwood Boulevard Temple, are displayed here. The windows depict the history of Judaism and were the result of the only LaFarge commission for a Jewish house of worship.

**35** ROCKHILL NEIGHBORHOOD, 46TH STREET TO PIERCE STREET AND LOCUST STREET TO TROOST AVENUE, 1901-1910. Developed by William Rockhill Nelson, co-founder of *The Kansas City Star,* this residential area reflects his affection for planned residential communities. Purchased in 1890, the land became the site of large homes constructed in a variety of popular architectural styles. Most were covered in clapboard or shingle siding with native limestone; many of these residences were occupied by Nelson's employees. Also notable in the neighborhood are the smaller homes along Brush Creek Boulevard and Pierce Street.

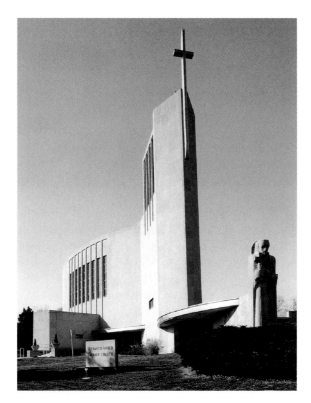

**36** ST. FRANCIS XAVIER CHURCH, 1001 E. 52ND STREET, 1950, BARRY BYRNE AND JOSEPH SHAUGHNESSY SR. This church is styled in the shape of a fish, an early religious symbol that represents followers of Jesus Christ. The simple exterior, geometric styling and absence of applied ornament are typical of modern design in the post-World War II era. A large sculpture by Alfonzo Ianelli stands in front of the church.

**37** MIDWEST RESEARCH INSTITUTE, 4801 ROCKHILL ROAD, 1951, NEVILLE, SHARP & SIMON; RENOVATION, 1999, RAFAEL ARCHITECTS. This research center borders the recently completed Brush Creek Cultural Corridor, and Theis Mall, a public plaza that contains one of the city's many fountains. Renovated in 1999, the building complex gained a new entrance and a perforated metal façade.

**38** EWING MARION KAUFFMAN FOUNDATION, 4801 ROCKHILL ROAD, 1999, KALLMAN, McKINNELL AND WOOD, BOSTON. This two-story building houses the headquarters of the Ewing Marion Kauffman Foundation, a prominent Midwestern philanthropic organization. Located on the center of 37 acres, the courtyard of this buff-colored brick and copper-roofed structure looks onto a man-made three-acre pond.

**39** EWING AND MURIEL KAUFFMAN MEMORIAL GARDENS, 4800 ROCKHILL ROAD, 2000, MAURICE JENNINGS AND FAY JONES; LANDSCAPING, MARSHALL TYLER RAUSCH. This memorial garden pays tribute to the Kauffmans and their involvement in the Kansas City community. The Visitors Center provides space for an information center and a state-of-the-art *orangery*, or conservatory, that contains many varieties of plants and flowers.

**40** KENNETH A. SPENCER CHEMISTRY AND BIOLOGY BUILDING, 50TH STREET AND ROCKHILL ROAD, 1972, KIVETT AND MYERS. The forms of this building emphasize large, geometric shapes and simple lines. The distinctive façade sharply contrasts with the older buildings on the University of Missouri–Kansas City campus.

**41** D.W. NEWCOMER'S SONS, 1331 BRUSH CREEK BOULEVARD, 1925, EDWARD BUEHLER DELK. An alternative to typical mortuary architecture, this Spanish-style building was built for one of the city's oldest businesses, founded in 1893. The building featured the first mortuary chapel in the city and a casket display room.

Brush Creek & Country Club

**42** VILLAGE GREEN APARTMENTS, 1500 E. 46TH STREET, 1949, HERBERT E. DUNCAN. These garden apartments were developed to help relieve the housing shortage that followed World War II. Their simple, Colonial Revival styling was typical of the era. Because the exterior wall materials vary from unit to unit, these apartments appear to be single-family row houses.

**43** PASEO ACADEMY OF VISUAL AND PERFORMING ARTS, 4747 FLORA AVENUE, 1992; HIGH SCHOOL, BNIM ARCHITECTS; MIDDLE SCHOOL, WRS ARCHITECTS. Built as the city's magnet school for the visual and performing arts, these brick structures provide a 1,200-seat auditorium, a 235-seat recital hall, a 135-seat black box theater, an art gallery and classroom space. The exteriors employ brick, playful white and blue tile designs and other materials that are resistant to deterioration.

**44** Swope Parkway Health Center, 3801 Blue Parkway, 1995, HNTB Architects. This facility houses the city's pre-eminent organization providing health care to the uninsured. Complimenting the brick façade are a large, rectangular tower and a curved, glass-covered entry.

**45** Bruce R. Watkins Cultural Heritage Center, 3700 Blue Parkway, 1989, By Design/Kansas City. This facility was designed to commemorate and celebrate the history of Kansas City's black community and its contributions to the city's growth and development. Its 250-seat theater is equipped for theatrical, oratory and visual productions while the gallery provides space to display the Foundation's collection of artifacts, art and the permanent exhibit on Bruce R. Watkins, who was a significant Kansas City area civic leader. The building is part of the cultural mall complex that consists of an amphitheater, the Satchel Paige Stadium and the *Spirit of Freedom* Fountain.

**46** BRUSH CREEK TOWERS APARTMENTS, 1800 BRUSH CREEK BOULEVARD, 1974, JOHN LAWRENCE DAW AND ASSOCIATES. Built as high-rise housing for the elderly, this structure contains a full-height interior court.

**47** CLEVELAND CHIROPRACTIC COLLEGE, 6401 ROCKHILL ROAD, 1954; ADDITION, 1963, LESLIE W. CORY. This structure originally housed a Church of the Nazarene and the auditorium retains original stained glass windows. The rectangular-box building offers three rows of fenestration on each of its four sides.

**48** KEMPER MUSEUM OF CONTEMPORARY ART, 4420 WARWICK BOULEVARD, 1994, GUNNAR BIRKERTS AND ASSOCIATES, INC. This museum of contemporary art contains a 22-foot-tall central skylit lobby and two wings that house offices, a meeting room, a sculpture courtyard, a café, a museum shop and an information area. The exterior materials are concrete, glass, granite and stainless steel. Louise Bourgeois' 1600-pound sculpture, *Spider, 1997*, greets visitors at the east entrance.

# Northwest

THE NORTHWEST DISTRICT OF THE KANSAS CITY metropolitan area rises north of the Missouri River and stretches from U.S. Highway 169 west and north to Interstate Highway 435.

Encompassing most of Platte County, the rich, rolling land near the Missouri has always been prime for agricultural development. Until recently, most of the area remained rural due to the fact that settlement historically occurred south of the river, near the communities of Westport and Independence. Remnants of plantation homes as well as farmhouses and cabins remain in the area.

After construction of the Kansas City International Airport in 1972, the metropolitan area began to sprawl northward. The local economies of northwest suburban "bedroom" communities, such as Weston, Riverside and Parkville, thrived as well. During the 1990s, the population increased more than 21 percent, reaching more than 70,000 residents. The tremendous growth of the area has been accompanied by beautification efforts, including the Northland Fountain at North Oak Trafficway and Vivion Road.

Northwest

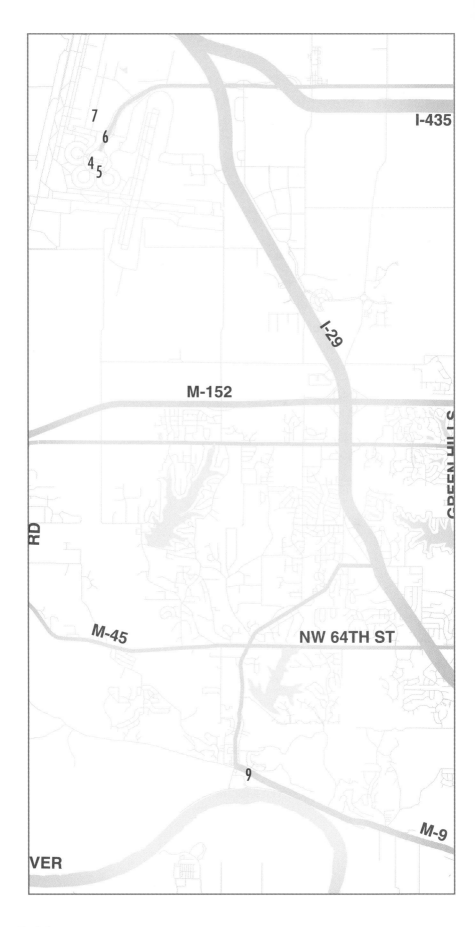

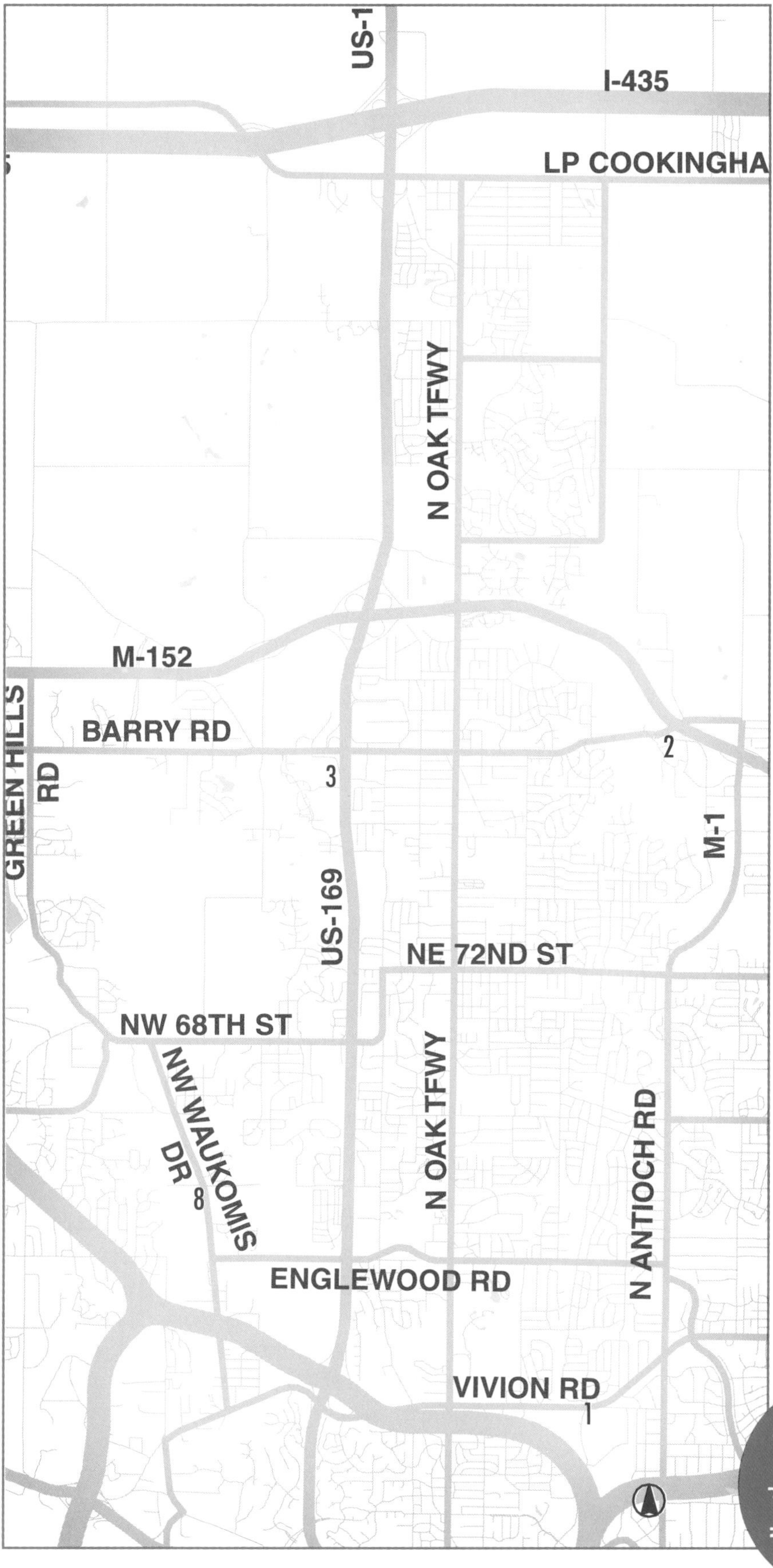
US-1
I-435
LP COOKINGHA
N OAK TFWY
M-152
BARRY RD
GREEN HILLS RD
2
3
M-1
US-169
NE 72ND ST
NW 68TH ST
NW WAUKOMIS DR
8
N OAK TFWY
N ANTIOCH RD
ENGLEWOOD RD
VIVION RD
1

Northwest

1 CLAY COUNTY ADMINISTRATIVE SERVICE CENTER, 1901 N.E. 48TH STREET, 1986, ABEND SINGLETON ASSOCIATES. This government building is recessed into the hillside and its terraced roof presents tiers of clerestory windows to provide extensive natural day lighting. The elongated floor plan features a series of retaining walls and porticos that unify the entire design.

2 MAPLE WOODS COMMUNITY COLLEGE, 2601 N.E. BARRY ROAD; FIRST PHASE, 1974, SELIGSON/EGGEN, INC. AND MARSHALL AND BROWN; SECOND PHASE, 1988, LINSCOTT HAYLETT WIMMER & WHEAT; NORTHLAND HUMAN SERVICES BUILDING ADDITION, 1995, FRANKHEISER AND HUTCHINS. Constructed in 1974, the Learning Resources building was the first structure on the college campus. The building incorporates interchangeable panels with windows and skylights to accommodate future growth. The designers were wise to plan for expansion; more than 15 buildings have been added to the original campus.

**3** NORTH PATROL DIVISION POLICE FACILITY, 1001 N.W. BARRY ROAD, 1978, DEVINE JAMES LABINSKI MYERS. The bright yellow metal panels that clad the exterior of this police station guarantee its visibility. The upper level houses offices, meeting facilities and a drive-through prisoner drop-off. The lower level contains detention facilities.

**4** KANSAS CITY INTERNATIONAL AIRPORT, INTERSTATE HIGHWAY 29 AND COOKINGHAM DRIVE, 1972, KIVETT AND MYERS. The airport's three-concourse design, one of the first in the nation, was designed by two of Kansas City's most active and widely known architects.

5 KANSAS CITY INTERNATIONAL AIRPORT ADMINISTRATION BUILDING, 1 INTERNATIONAL SQUARE, 1972, KIVETT AND MYERS. Designed in International style, this building sits in the center of the three-terminal airport complex.

6 THREE FIGURES/FIFTEEN ELEMENTS, JOEL SHAPIRO, KANSAS CITY INTERNATIONAL AIRPORT, COOKINGHAM DRIVE, 1996, BRONZE, 18' (ABOVE LEFT), 15' (ABOVE RIGHT), 24' (RIGHT). Often the first pieces of Kansas City sculpture that visitors experience, these three bronze figurative pieces are located in the native prairie grass preserve near the Kansas City International Airport.

7 AVIATION DEPARTMENT ADMINISTRATION BUILDING, 601 BRASILIA AVENUE, 1995, CDFM² ARCHITECTURE. This two-story building includes the main office facility, utility garage space and training center. Trelliswork that aligns with vertically oriented glazing systems "punched" into the pre-cast concrete façade distinguish the west side of this building.

**8** RIVERSIDE COMMUNITY CENTER, 5940 N.W. WAUKOMIS ROAD, 1998, WRS ARCHITECTS, INC. Located in a rapidly expanding suburb, this 16,400 square-foot community center contains meeting rooms, a gymnasium, a serving kitchen and a performance stage. The exterior elements include brick, glass and metal, exposed steel trusses and geometric building layers.

**9** MACKAY HALL, PARK UNIVERSITY, 8700 N.W.
RIVER PARK DRIVE, 1891, MASTER BUILDER,
PATRICK BREEN; RENOVATION, 1994, WRS
ARCHITECTS, INC. As a means of earning their
tuition, 300 inexperienced student builders,
under the close supervision of a master
builder, Patrick Breen, provided the
labor for the construction of this Park
University symbol. Their tasks included
excavating, quarrying and transporting
limestone, milling lumber and constructing
the building. Located atop a hill that
overlooks the Missouri River, this Victorian-
style building features a pitched roof, gabled
dormers, a clock tower and white and tan
native limestone. In the early 1980s, one of
the turrets was damaged in a thunderstorm
and in 1994, an elevator was installed and
the interior was completely renovated to
improve accessibility.

# B Northeast

ORDERING THE MIGHTY MISSOURI RIVER AND encompassing more than half of Clay County, the northeast section of the Kansas City metropolitan area reaches north to U.S. Highway 92 and from U.S. Highway 169 east past U.S. Highway 33.

The Northeast offers rolling hills and fertile soil where game was once plentiful and Native Americans were the primary inhabitants. The area attracted pioneers and fur trappers such as Daniel Morgan Boone and, in 1821, François Chouteau, who later established the settlement where Kansas City, Missouri, began. In 1869, the Hannibal Bridge first connected the north and south banks of the Missouri River; this bridge signaled the arrival of railroads and the area's growth into the Midwest's largest transportation and commercial center.

As a result of their proximity to the railroads and Kansas City, communities near the river, such as Gladstone, North Kansas City and Claycomo, became industrial towns. Liberty, established around 1817, boasts one of the top liberal arts colleges in the Midwest, William Jewell College, and the Olde Towne Square, c.1888, a national historic landmark.

The Northeast is a thriving park and entertainment district. Once called "Kansas City's biggest secret," the Northeast is growing at a steady rate — more than 30,000 residents moved there in the 1990s.

155

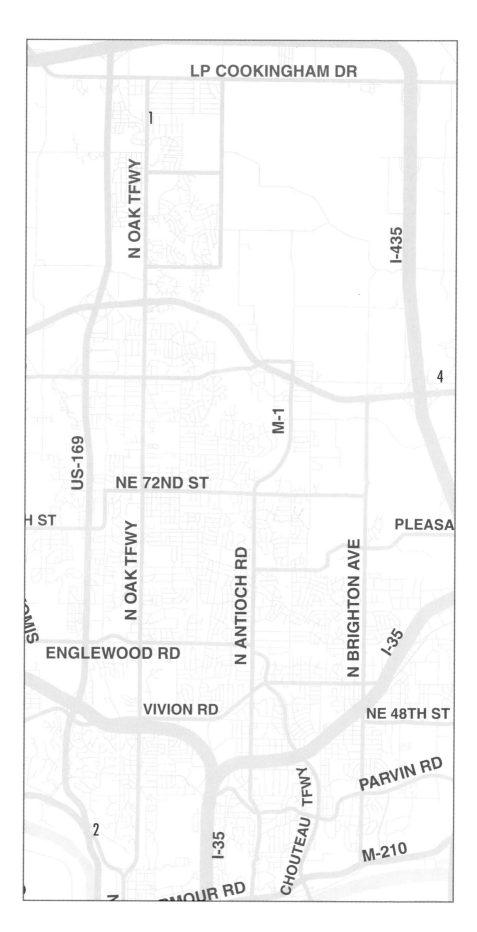

LP COOKINGHAM DR

1

N OAK TFWY

I-435

4

M-1

US-169

NE 72ND ST

H ST

PLEASA

N OAK TFWY

N ANTIOCH RD

N BRIGHTON AVE

I-35

ENGLEWOOD RD

VIVION RD

NE 48TH ST

SIMS

PARVIN RD

CHOUTEAU TFWY

2

I-35

M-210

MOUR RD

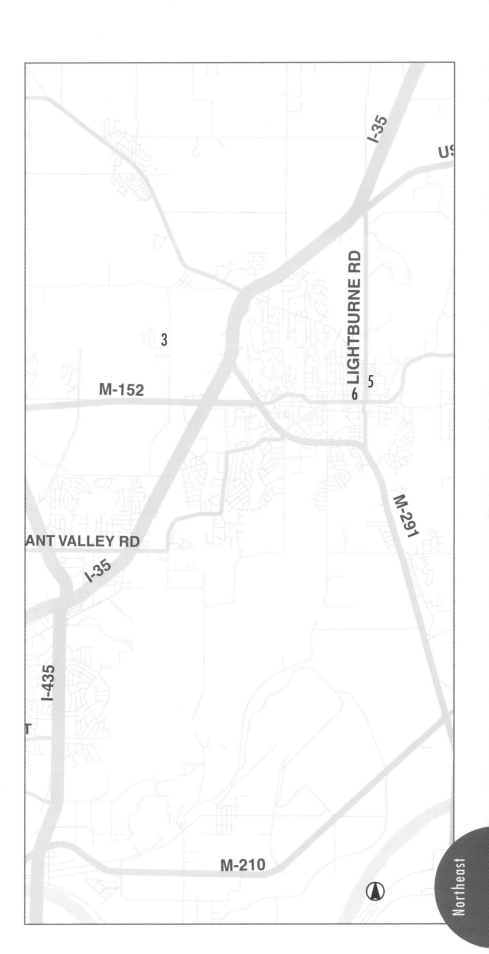

M-152

3

LIGHTBURNE RD

I-35

US

5
6

M-291

ANT VALLEY RD

I-35

I-435

T

M-210

1 KANSAS CITY, MISSOURI, FIRE DEPARTMENT STATION NO. 3, 11101 NORTH OAK STREET, 1998, SHAUGHNESSY FICKEL & SCOTT. Designed with a sense of traditional fire stations, this example provides sleeping areas on the second level and brass sliding poles. Glazed towers bring natural light into the station by day and provide light for the neighborhood at night.

2 RESIDENCE, FRANK BOTT, 3640 BRIARCLIFF ROAD, 1959, FRANK LLOYD WRIGHT. One of Frank Lloyd Wright's last homes, this house follows his maxim, "No house should be built on a hill. It should be of the hill." The structure repeats geometric patterns and features natural exterior elements including concrete, stone and wood in earth- and sky-tone hues. The terrace allows a 180-degree view that captures the Kansas City skyline and the Missouri River. In 1980, Wright was awarded the "Architectural Excellence in Retrospect Award" from the Kansas City chapter of the American Institute of Architects for this masterpiece.

**3** Residence, Elbridge Arnold, 8900 N.E. Flintlock Street, 1856, architect unknown. This Greek Revival-style farmhouse is known as "Woodneath" because of the many shade trees that surround it. Eighteen-inch-thick walls of handmade brick rest on a native limestone foundation.

**4** Hodge Park Shelter, 7000 N.E. Barry Road, 1994, International Architects Atelier. This amphitheater features a fan-shaped seating area that provides clear and unobstructed views for all spectators. Twelve partial trusses covered with a layer of copper constitute the dome.

5 LIBERTY SQUARE, BOUNDED BY MISSOURI, GALLATIN AND MILL STREETS. First settled in 1817, Liberty became the Clay County seat in 1822. The square retains numerous 19th-century commercial buildings; more than 30 of these historic buildings are on the National Register of Historic Places. A prominent Civil War soldier and William Jewell supporter, Alexander Doniphan led the longest march in United States military history from Liberty Square to the battlefields of the Mexican-American War in 1846.

Overlooking Liberty Square is WILLIAM JEWELL COLLEGE, one of the oldest private colleges in Missouri. Founded by the Baptists of Missouri in 1849, the college is located on 149 wooded and hilly acres. One of the original trustees was the Rev. Robert James, father of Jesse James. William Jewell, a doctor and philanthropist from Columbia, Missouri, gave $10,000 to help open the school, but he died of heat stroke while overseeing the construction of Jewell Hall (above) in 1853. During the Civil War, this structure housed wounded Union troops and their horses. Today the college is one of the region's leading liberal arts colleges.

**6** CLAY COUNTY GOVERNMENT CENTER AND JAMES S. ROONEY JUSTICE CENTER, 11-14 S. WATER ROAD, 1986, ABEND SINGLETON ASSOCIATES. This mixed-use complex is located on the new civic plaza, which creates a visual relationship between the old and the new courthouses. Exterior materials include limestone and brick. Stylized windows imitate the surrounding historic buildings; ceramic murals, designed by Matthew Monk, celebrate the community's history. The justice section of the building has a monumental entrance portal with flanking columns.

# S Southeast

OUTH OF 63RD STREET IN KANSAS CITY, MISSOURI, lies a group of small neighborhoods and suburbs that extend from the Kansas-Missouri border east to the town of Lee's Summit and south to the edge of the metropolitan area.

As Kansas City became a popular industrial and commercial center, its population and residential neighborhoods grew. Though the area southeast of the city center retained many farms and orchards into the early 20th century, Kansas City's population spread as communities including Waldo, Dodson and Dallas formed in the southern district and towns such as Lee's Summit expanded. Many homes were built between the 1920s and the 1970s that featured bungalow, ranch and split-level residential architecture.

Today, the Southeast boasts many fine examples of architectural innovation and endurance including the Truman Sports Complex, one of the earliest and best dual sports stadiums in the nation; Unity Village, a religious complex that features Mediterranean-style buildings and fountains; the Longview Farm, the summer estate of a local lumber magnate; and Alexander Majors' house, where wagon trains stopped and the Pony Express was born.

Southeast

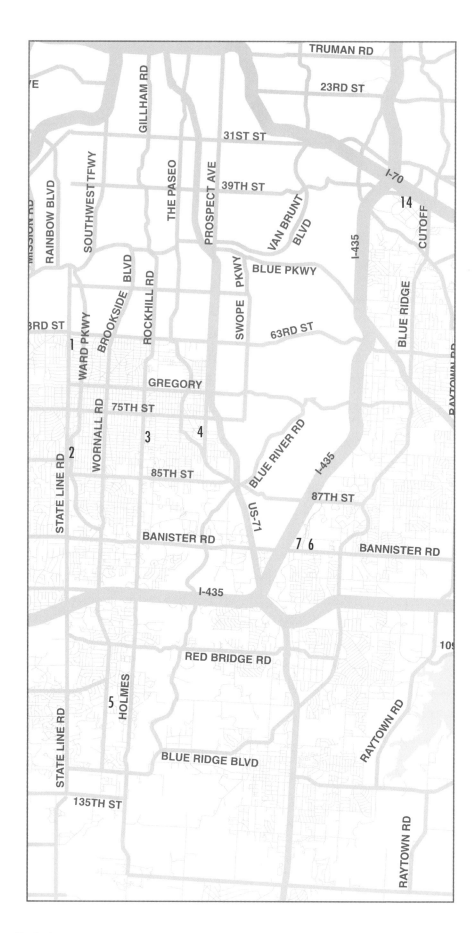

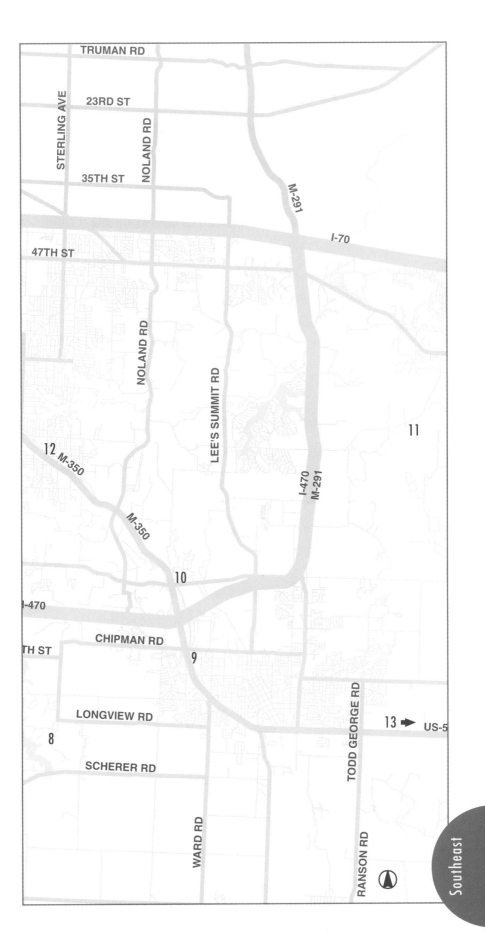

TRUMAN RD

STERLING AVE

23RD ST

NOLAND RD

35TH ST

M-291

I-70

47TH ST

NOLAND RD

LEE'S SUMMIT RD

11

12 M-350

I-470
M-291

M-350

10

I-470

CHIPMAN RD

TH ST

9

LONGVIEW RD

TODD GEORGE RD

13 ➡ US-5

8

SCHERER RD

WARD RD

RANSON RD

Southeast

1 RESIDENCE, WALTER E. BIXBY, 6505 STATE LINE ROAD, 1937, EDWARD W. TANNER. This two-story mansion is the earliest example of International-style architecture in Kansas City. The style of the exterior reflects the influence of Le Corbusier and features a concrete and stucco façade, terraces and cantilevered balconies supported by steel columns.

2 RESIDENCE, ALEXANDER MAJORS, 8145 STATE LINE ROAD, 1856, ARCHITECT UNKNOWN; ADDITIONS, c.1903, ARCHITECT UNKNOWN; RESTORATION, 1984, TERRY CHAPMAN. This house is the third-oldest structure in Kansas City and is one of the earliest wood frame Revival-style homes in the area. It was also one of the first houses in the area to have closets and to use "extravagant" glass windows. It is most noteworthy for its historical association with Alexander Majors, field coordinator for Russell, Majors & Waddell, founders of the Pony Express. Their firm was instrumental in transforming Westport Landing, the origin of Kansas City, into the main Midwestern hub for transportation of commercial freight to the Western frontier. Majors was responsible for safely leading many successful wagon trains across the Santa Fe Trail and gave "Buffalo Bill" Cody his first job as a Pony Express rider.

**3** SHALOM PLAZA APARTMENTS, 7777 HOLMES STREET, 1977, ABEND SINGLETON ASSOCIATES. A Housing and Urban Development government project, this building features a six-story, glass-lined atrium that allows an abundance of natural light into the central corridor of the building.

**4** FIRE STATION NO. 30, 7534 PROSPECT AVENUE, 1970, SELIGSON/EGGEN, INC. Much of this unusual fire station is enclosed by glass panels, and the fire trucks and equipment are on display to the public. However, masonry covers the two side wings.

**5** GREEK ORTHODOX CHURCH OF THE ANNUNCIATION, 12001 WORNALL ROAD, 1974, THE RAMOS GROUP. Exterior features such as the raised dome, the striped brick and the decorative cross placed on the east wall create a modern expression of Greek Orthodox religious motifs.

**6** HILLCREST BANK OFFICE BUILDING, 5800 E. BANNISTER ROAD, 1988, ABEND SINGLETON ASSOCIATES. This black, glass-box office building is a minimalist composition constructed of stone and large architectural elements.

**7** INSPIRATION, RITA BLITT, 5800 E. BANNISTER ROAD, 1987, STAINLESS STEEL, 26′ x 18″ x 18′. Commissioned by the building's architect, this abstract sculpture depicts a stainless steel figure dancing on a stone embankment. Its image is multiplied in the reflective surfaces of the Hillcrest Bank building to create a troupe that appears to dance through the site as motorists pass.

**8** Longview Farm, 3361 S.W. Longview Road, 1914, Henry F. Hoit.
The weekend retreat of Robert A. Long, a Kansas City lumber baron, this estate was described as a rural Versailles — a complex of 40 structures, including a country mansion, barns and housing for workers. Hoit, a noted Kansas City architect, combined frame construction with cream-colored stucco walls, red tile roofing and classical motifs on most of the buildings to create a unified style. The buildings were designed to include the latest in technological advances such as underground connections for water and sewers, electricity and steam heating.

The 1650-acre property was equipped with seven miles of rock roads, two miles of formal drives, and a 20-acre artificial lake. The landscape surrounding the mansion held formal gardens that contained pergolas, sunken gardens, fountains and tapestry brick retaining walls. A show barn, a half-mile racetrack, a grandstand and a clubhouse accommodated the training, breeding and racing of Hackney horses and other champion livestock. Loula Long Combs, daughter of R.A. Long, became a successful American Saddlebred horse rider and was one of the top horsewomen in the United States for many years.

Beginning in 1963, many buildings were demolished and much of the land redeveloped for new uses. Loula Long Combs and her sister, Sallie Long Ellis, donated 146 acres to establish Longview Community College in 1964. The Army Corps of Engineers flooded 950 acres of the estate to create Longview Lake. The mansion, some gardens, the show barn and a few other buildings remain in their original condition and are used for weddings, retreats, parties, fund-raisers and corporate meetings.

Southeast

**9** SUMMIT PARK PLAZA, U.S. HIGHWAY 50 AND PARK LANE, 1974, COLLABORATIVE: PHASE ONE PLUS. This one-story office complex was a creative solution to a limited design budget. Brick walls accented by circular openings create courtyards for each storefront while also allowing natural light to reach the offices.

**10** UNITY VILLAGE, 1901 N.W. BLUE PARKWAY, 1929, BOILLOT & LAUCK; ADDITION, 1949, RICKERT FILLMORE; ACTIVITY CENTER AND UNITY INN ADDITIONS, 1975, LINSCOTT HAYLETT; SILENT UNITY BUILDING ADDITION, 1989, HNTB ARCHITECTS; ADMINISTRATIVE BUILDING ADDITION AND RENOVATION, 1996, HANSEN MIDGELY & NIEMACKL. In 1920, Charles and Myrtle Fillmore founded the Unity School of Christianity and, in 1921, the first buildings, English Cottage homes, were built and utilized on the site. By 1949, the Mediterranean-style tower, Silent Unity Building, and administration and classroom buildings were added to the 1,400-acre campus. Built entirely by Unity workers, the complex has many design innovations including storage of 100,000 gallons of water in the bell tower, underground utility placement and a cooling system that utilizes outdoor water fountains.

**11** NORTH DOCK OBSERVATION PLATFORM, 22807 WOODS CHAPEL ROAD, 1961, ELPIDIO ROCHA. Steel beams and limestone-clad columns support this innovative, covered dock.

**12** MISSOURI PUBLIC SERVICE CORPORATE HEADQUARTERS, 10700 E. HIGHWAY 50, 1958, KIVETT AND MYERS AND McCALLUM. This office building was one of the first structures in the area to utilize energy-conserving materials. Mechanical louvers control sun absorption, reducing energy requirements for cooling the building.

Southeast

**13** VISITORS EDUCATION CENTER AND MARJORIE POWELL ALLEN CHAPEL, POWELL GARDENS, 1609 N.W. U.S. HIGHWAY 50, 1994, FAY JONES AND MAURICE JENNINGS, ARCHITECTS. Since 1988, Powell Gardens, a non-profit horticultural foundation, has developed beautiful botanical gardens on its 835-acre property. The centerpiece of the gardens, the Visitors Education Center, is a T-shaped structure covered with wood shingles and siding, glass panels, limestone, and topped with low-slope, shallow-hip roofs. Surrounded by large formal gardens, the southern wing features a glass-covered *orangery*, or greenhouse, that allows plant life to flourish year-round. Located at the edge of the gardens' lake, the Marjorie Powell Allen Chapel reflects the natural beauty that surrounds it. The structure has natural rock floors, glass wall panels and natural wood supports that allow light to flow through the building. Wood beams compose the Gothic-style roof, interlocking to form open-diamond patterns.

**14** Harry S. Truman Sports Complex, 8501 Stadium Drive, 1972-1973, Charles Deaton with Kivett and Myers, HNTB Architects. Funded by a $43 million bond issue in 1968, Kauffman and Arrowhead Stadiums were designed to house the Kansas City Royals and the Kansas City Chiefs, respectively. The architects were among the first to create these unique back-to-back concrete stadiums with facilities tailored to each sport. National television and radio broadcasters regularly tout the quality of the structures' design.

MAST ADVERTISING & PUBLISHING

# Southwest

LOCATED IN THE SOUTHWEST CORNER OF THE GREATER Kansas City metropolitan area, Johnson County, Kansas, was named for the Rev. Thomas Johnson, who opened a mission school for Shawnee Indians who were forced by the federal government to relocate to the Kansas Territory.

During the last decade of the 19th century, William Strang built an interurban railroad from Kansas City to Olathe in the central part of Johnson County and developed the first Overland Park subdivision. Economic success and changing population patterns in Kansas City, Missouri, prompted the desire for additional residential space in the area. Johnson County grew with increasing numbers of popular suburban "bedroom" communities. Early among these, the J.C. Nichols Company planned and developed Mission Hills as an affluent Kansas residential district.

After World War II, the federal government developed programs that enabled middle-class families to more easily purchase homes within the suburban neighborhoods. As a result, new residential subdivisions were built quickly and families filled the developments. Planned commercial centers, such as Corporate Woods, began in the late 1970s and spurred additional residential development. In the year 2000, the Johnson County population had reached nearly 450,000.

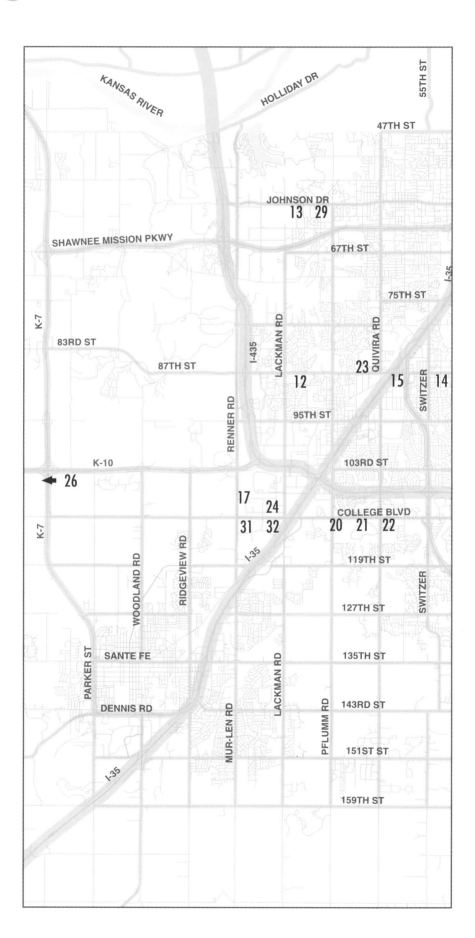

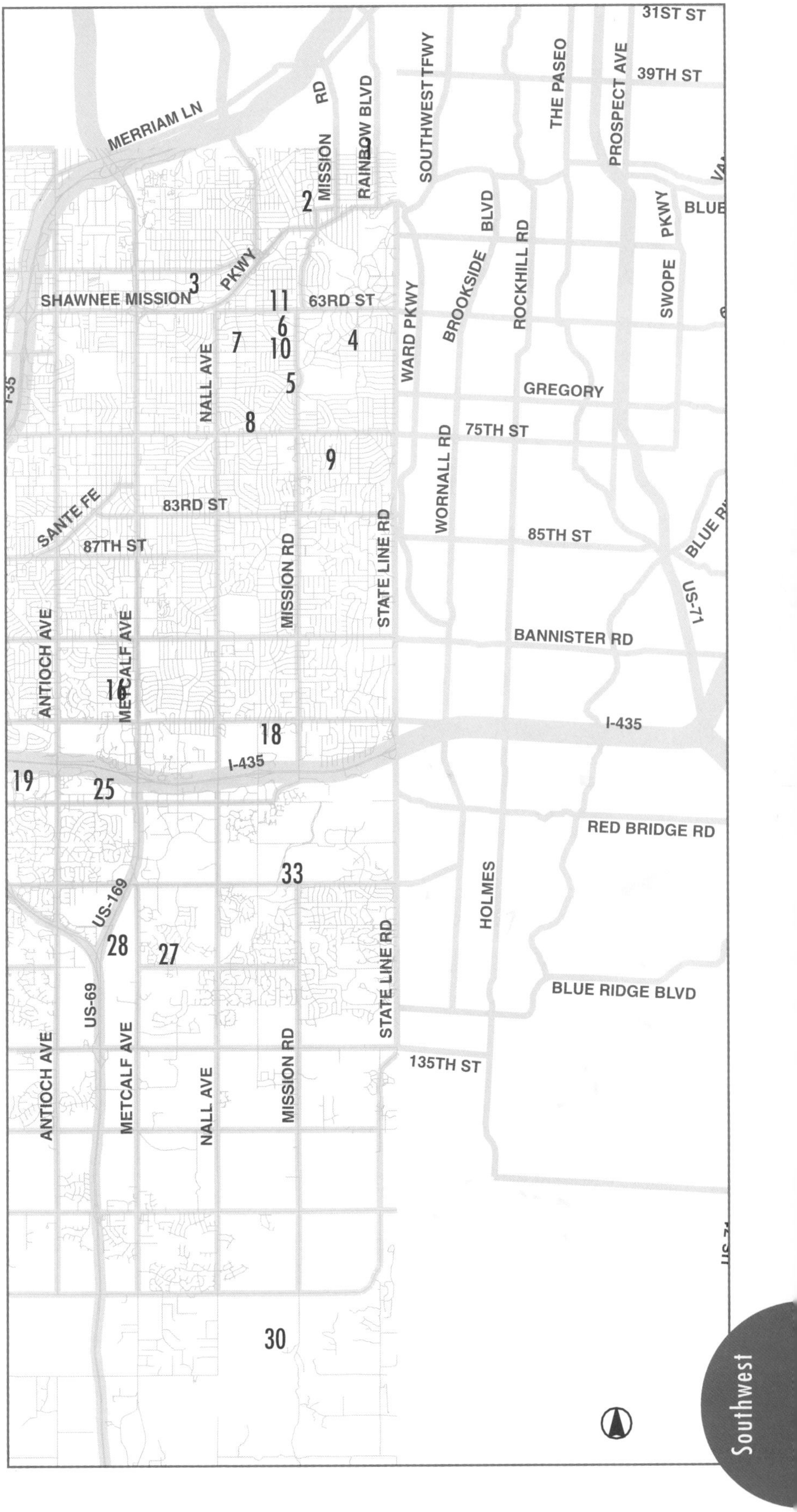

31ST ST
39TH ST
MERRIAM LN
MISSION RD
RAINBOW BLVD
SOUTHWEST TFWY
THE PASEO
PROSPECT AVE
2
SHAWNEE MISSION
PKWY
3
11
63RD ST
BROOKSIDE BLVD
ROCKHILL RD
BLUE
SWOPE PKWY
WARD PKWY
7
6
10
4
NALL AVE
5
GREGORY
8
WORNALL RD
75TH ST
9
SANTE FE
83RD ST
87TH ST
MISSION RD
STATE LINE RD
85TH ST
BLUE R
US-71
ANTIOCH AVE
METCALF AVE
BANNISTER RD
16
I-435
18
I-435
RED BRIDGE RD
19
25
US-169
33
HOLMES
28
27
US-69
STATE LINE RD
BLUE RIDGE BLVD
ANTIOCH AVE
METCALF AVE
NALL AVE
MISSION RD
135TH ST
30

Southwest

1 WESTWOOD CITY HALL, 4700 RAINBOW BOULEVARD, 1991, BNIM ARCHITECTS. This 16,000 square-foot community building is constructed of red brick, synthetic stucco and concrete masonry and houses council chambers, a courtroom, a multi-purpose community room, and a police facility.

2 SHAWNEE INDIAN MISSION, 3403 W. 53RD STREET, 1841, ARCHITECT UNKNOWN. Established by Rev. Thomas Johnson as a Methodist mission, the structures were part of a residential school where Native American children were taught English, manual arts and agriculture. At one time, the mission and the school maintained 16 buildings, fields, orchards and pastures. In 1927, the state purchased the property, and the Kansas State Historical Society maintains period rooms that are open to the public.

**3** FINE ARTS THEATER, 5909 JOHNSON DRIVE, 1938, IRA WHEELER. This movie theater is of poured concrete construction. Painted linear and geometric Art Deco ornamentation decorates the theater's brick walls and entrance.

**4** RESIDENCE, 67TH STREET AND BELINDER AVENUE, 1957, MARCEL BREUER. An American adaptation of Bauhaus philosophy, this functional residence combines the structure and aethestics into one form.

**5** PRAIRIE VILLAGE SHOPPING CENTER, 3920 W. 69TH TERRACE AT MISSION ROAD, 1948, EDWARD TANNER. Like Crestwood and the Country Club Plaza, this shopping center was built by J.C. Nichols to provide a central shopping area for one of his residential neighborhoods. Tanner, who designed Crestwood and sections of the Plaza, used Spanish-style architecture, decorative tile and landscaping to give the shopping center a distinctive character.

**6** RESIDENCES, 3909-4104 DELMAR DRIVE, c.1960. Located adjacent to a local country club, this grouping of one-level, contemporary Ranch-style houses is typical of local housing developments constructed during the 1960s.

7 RESIDENCE, 5020 W. 67TH STREET, 1966, BRUCE GOFF. This residence is one of four Goff residences in the metropolitan area. Renowned for his eccentric designs, Goff utilized geometric shapes and details in this structure. Most unusual is the interior design which features open spaces and a tall central roof with skylights.

8 RESIDENCES, 7334-7356 ROE CIRCLE, 1949, DAVID RUNNELLS. Developed by Donald Drummond, these split-level, wood and brick-trimmed houses provide residents outdoor yard space around a park at 7342 Roe Circle.

9 RESIDENCES, 77TH TO 79TH STREETS, CANTERBURY TO CHADWICK DRIVES, c.1950, DONALD DRUMMOND, DEVELOPER AND BUILDER. Designed in the contemporary California style, this group of houses features covered garages and walkways, sloping roofs and wood siding.

Southwest

**10** PRAIRIE ELEMENTARY SCHOOL, 6642 MISSION ROAD, 1993, GOULD EVANS ASSOCIATES. After fire damaged one of the oldest and most historically significant schools in Johnson County, this 63,000 square-foot facility was built to replace it. The design of the new structure features expandable "education pods" and incorporates salvaged elements from the old school.

**11** CONSOLIDATED FIRE DISTRICT NO. 2 HEADQUARTERS, NORTHEAST JOHNSON COUNTY FIRE STATION NO. 2, 3921 W. 63RD STREET, 1999, SHAUGHNESSY FICKEL & SCOTT ARCHITECTS. Located in a residential area, this state-of-the-art 13,158 square-foot facility replaced a 1940s vintage fire station. The apparatus bays are surrounded by ancillary support functions and form a raised, asymmetrical "butterfly" roof. Natural light from the bays illuminates the firehouse from the south and shields its front apron. The district headquarters are separate from the station but linked to it through shared design features including pre-cast vertical fins and exposed structural-steel at the entries and above the apparatus bays.

**12** INDIAN TRAILS SWIMMING POOL, 8801 GREENWAY LANE, SAR-KO-PAR PARK, c.1960, ARCHITECT UNKNOWN; RENOVATION, 1998, SHAUGHNESSY FICKEL & SCOTT ARCHITECTS. This renovation project included remodeling the vintage pool; adding a new deck, a curved, zero-depth beach area and two water slides; and relocating shade structures, the bathhouse and concession area. The aluminum bathhouse roof and shade structures are supported by galvanized steel columns and tie rods that imitate sailboat masts at port.

**13** BROKEN ARROW ELEMENTARY SCHOOL, 6301 ALDEN ROAD, 1990, ABEND SINGLETON ASSOCIATES. Located in a community rich in Native American history and named after the Indian symbol for peace, the design of this elementary school combines history, innovative technology and artful designs. The building is divided in three sections including the "village" where individual sculptural buildings are centrally placed; the academic wing where classrooms surround the research center; and the "forum" where special events are held.

Southwest

183

**14** JOHNSON COUNTY CENTRAL RESOURCE LIBRARY RENOVATION, 9875 W. 87TH STREET, 1993, GOULD EVANS ASSOCIATES. To accommodate increasing patronage, the Johnson County Library commissioned the renovation of an abandoned 80,000 square-foot retail store and construction of a 6,000 square-foot addition. To capture natural light for the windowless existing building, the façade was torn off and daylight was brought in through glazed walls and ceilings.

**15** UNITED MISSOURI BANK, 87TH STREET AND NIEMAN ROAD, 1997, JOHN LAWRENCE DAW & ASSOCIATES AND INTERNATIONAL ARCHITECTS ATELIER. This unusual drive-up banking facility includes a cone-shaped teller building and a triangular slab that covers the seven lanes and ATM kiosks.

**16** ATONEMENT LUTHERAN CHURCH, 9948 METCALF AVENUE, 1997, SHAUGHNESSY FICKEL & SCOTT ARCHITECTS. Nestled into a sloping site, this brick-clad religious complex has a prominent central entrance supported by brick and steel columns and accented by a stepped brick tower and a decorative cross panel. The roof structure, which covers the worship space and allows natural light to bathe the nave, consists of simple, layered beams and is fronted by glass windows.

**17** FIRE STATION NO. 4, 10855 EICHER DRIVE, 1990, SHAUGHNESSY FICKEL & SCOTT ARCHITECTS. The station contains three functional sections — apparatus storage, ancillary station support and living quarters. White stucco encases the curved storage bays, white louvered forms house the mechanical units, and masonry and large punched window openings cover the living quarters. A block wall extends from the building center in conjunction with horizontal steel canopies at two entrances.

**18** KANTER HOUSE, 11 WYCKLOW, 1971, ABEND SINGLETON ASSOCIATES. Built on a hill, this residence features brick walls and chateau-like sloping roofs made up of materials that reflect the surrounding landscape.

**19** CORPORATE WOODS, ANTIOCH ROAD TO OVERLAND PARKWAY AND INTERSTATE HIGHWAY 435 TO COLLEGE BOULEVARD, 1974-1979, MARSHALL AND BROWN; LANDSCAPING, SWA GROUP. During the 1970s, this large complex  developed as an alternative to office locations in the urban core and in commercial strips adjacent to residential neighborhoods. Located on a 300-acre, wooded site, the complex has grown from the original 12 buildings to more than 25.

**20** JOHNSON COUNTY COMMUNITY COLLEGE, 12345 COLLEGE BOULEVARD, 1971; ADDITIONS, 1982; MARSHALL AND BROWN. Located on 240 acres and originally placed around a courtyard, this college complex now includes 13 buildings due to the steady increase of the student population. The brown brick buildings utilize geometric designs and are surrounded by art from the school's sculpture collection.

**21** THE CARLSEN CENTER, JOHNSON COUNTY COMMUNITY COLLEGE, 12345 COLLEGE BOULEVARD, 1990, PGAV ARCHITECTS. The Carlsen Center serves as the new gateway to the Johnson County Community College campus and also as the location for arts and entertainment events and education. The Center includes a 1400-seat multipurpose theater, a 400-seat drama theater, a 100-seat black box theater, a recital hall and an art gallery.

Southwest

**22** JOHNSON COUNTY COMMUNITY COLLEGE/OPPENHEIMER-STEIN SCULPTURE COLLECTION, 12345 COLLEGE BOULEVARD, 1990. The college's 234-acres of rolling hills, courtyards and buildings provide an ideal backdrop for its contemporary sculpture collection. The Oppenheimer-Stein Sculpture Collection has expanded by adding important pieces by Louise Bourgeois and Jonathan Borofsky. Louise Bourgeois' *Woman with Packages* (top), 1996, is composed of wood cast in bronze. As Bourgeois notes, the sculpture is a portrait of herself with her sons. Located on the roof of the COM Building, Jonathon Borofsky's *Walking Man (On The Edge)* (bottom), 1995, is made of fiberglass and steel. Borofsky's interest in the linear and conceptual is well represented in this piece.

**23** CITY HALL, LENEXA, KANSAS, ADDITION AND RENOVATION, 12350 WEST 87TH STREET PARKWAY, 1996, SHAUGHNESSY FICKEL & SCOTT ARCHITECTS. The addition and renovation processes have produced a central corridor that links the buildings' elements to enhance the sense of unity. These elements include a water fountain, a courtyard, a public lobby and the civic rotunda.

**24** JOHN A. MARSHALL COMPANY OFFICES, 10930 LACKMAN ROAD, 1979, ARCHITECT UNKNOWN; RENOVATION, 1996, SHAUGHNESSY FICKEL & SCOTT ARCHITECTS. The exterior cladding of this building features white metal panels and aluminum trim. Originally built to house an industrial camera headquarters, a furniture dealer purchased the building in 1996 and transformed it into a warehouse. Additions included enclosures, skylights and open showrooms.

**25** 7500 W. 110TH STREET BUILDING, 1984, PBNI ARCHITECTS. The former MAST Corporate Headquarters consists of two blocks of offices connected by a vertical circulation core. The roof projects over the body of the brick building and shades the six stories below.

**26** LOOKING THROUGH, SHAUN CASSIDY, CEDAR CREEK DEVELOPMENT, HIDDEN LAKES PARK, 103RD STREET AND HIDDEN LAKES NORTH, 1999, CONCRETE AND WOOD, 7' x 20' x 40'. Commissioned for the Cedar Creek residential community, *Looking Through* is located in a wooded portion of the nearby park and is accessible by footpath. Sculpted of structurally reinforced concrete, the piece is an abstract representation of home and family.

**27** CONGREGATION BETH TORAH RELIGIOUS FACILITY, 6100 W. 127TH STREET, 1996, GOULD EVANS GOODMAN ASSOCIATES AND SOLOMON ASSOCIATES. This monumental structure incorporates white stone walls to suggest the walls of Jerusalem. Seven steel columns, symbolizing the columns in the Old Testament tabernacle, support the massive 60-foot ceiling coffer, the curving walls and the glass panels in the 400-seat sanctuary.

**28** W. JACK SANDERS JUSTICE CENTER, 12400 FOSTER DRIVE, 1997, GOULD EVANS GOODMAN ASSOCIATES. A two-story arcade, which links the departments of this government building, can expand to connect with future additions. As a result, the façade provides open access at several points along the arcade.

Southwest

**29** SHAWNEE BRANCH LIBRARY, 13811 JOHNSON DRIVE, 1992, GOULD EVANS ASSOCIATES. Resting on a heavily wooded hillside, this 15,000 square-foot library takes advantage of the surrounding landscape. The back of the building is a glass wall that allows patrons an excellent view of the outdoor scenery.

**30** BLUE VALLEY MIDDLE SCHOOL, 4601 W. 163RD TERRACE, 1998, GOULD EVANS GOODMAN ASSOCIATES. The design divides the school into districts whose construction materials suggest the purpose of each exploratory classroom. The "art district" features burnished concrete, stained wood and tile, while materials such as metal panel and concrete block clad the "industrial district."

**31** MAHAFFIE HOUSE, 1100 N. KANSAS CITY ROAD, 1858; ADDITIONS, 1865, 1895; ARCHITECT(S) UNKNOWN; RENOVATION, 1982, PBNI ARCHITECTS. This house was an early stop on the Santa Fe Trail. After the complete restoration of the historic landmark, the City of Olathe began operating the facility as the Mahaffie Stagecoach Stop & Farm Museum.

**32** Lackman Thompson Farmhouse, 11180 Lackman Road, 1887, William Lackman; renovation, 1997, Black & Veatch. William Lackman, a farmer and developer of the Kansas City/Olathe interurban electric railway, built this three-story residence in Second Empire and Queen Anne architectural styles and even brought European craftsmen to construct the elaborate interior woodwork. In 1908, Frank Thompson, a mule and horse dealer, purchased the farm, including all the additional structures, equipment and livestock for $32,000. The Lenexa Chamber of Commerce is now housed in this historic structure.

**33** Church of the Nativity, 2800 W. 119th Street, 1992, Shaughnessy Fickel & Scott. This church features a limestone base with high exterior stucco walls accented by tall narrow windows that pierce the roof line. The structure houses a 1,000-seat, light-diffused worship space, a small daily chapel, a meeting space, and a parish hall and offices located below the worship space.

Southwest

# Independence, Missouri

LOCATED IN THE NORTHEAST PORTION OF THE metropolitan area near the Missouri River, Independence, Missouri, was the westernmost settlement in the United States at the time of its founding. By 1826, it had become the Jackson County seat and the commercial center for the agricultural goods that were produced in the area. The original starting point of the Santa Fe Trail, by 1832 it had become a significant outfitting hub for travelers bound for Mexico, Oregon and California. Independence lost its pre-eminence as the primary outfitting center and starting point for the Santa Fe Trail after the founding of Westport.

In 1830-31, members of the Church of Jesus Christ of Latter-day Saints moved into Independence, establishing schools, stores, a ferry, churches and two newspapers. Although the Mormons were forced out of Jackson County in 1833, they returned in 1886 as the Reorganized Church of Jesus Christ of Latter-day Saints. The world headquarters of the church, renamed the Community of Christ in 2000, is still located here.

In 1885 a boulevard and railroads connected Independence to Kansas City, and it became a popular residential suburb, filled with many lovely Victorian houses. Today, the city is well-known as the hometown of Harry S. Truman, the 33rd president of the United States, who believed that "Independence is the best place in the world."

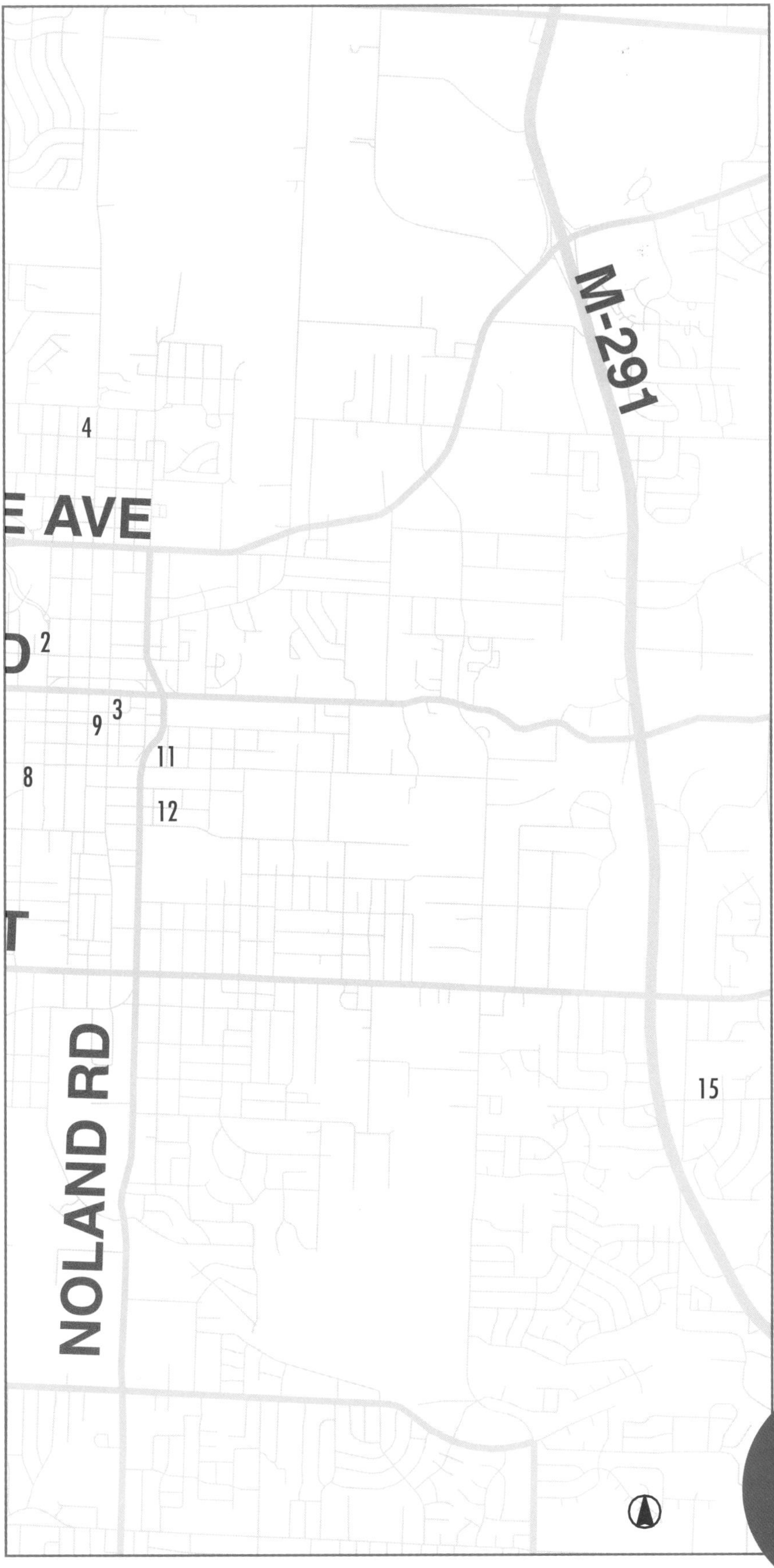
M-291
4
E AVE
D
2
3
9
11
8
12
T
NOLAND RD
15

1 RESIDENCE, NOLAND WHITE, 1024 S. FOREST STREET, c.1850, ARCHITECT UNKNOWN. Smallwood Noland, a leader in the expulsion of the Church of Jesus Christ of Latter-day Saints in 1833, commissioned this I-plan home with Greek Revival elements, including cornice returns in the gable ends and classical treatment of the central bay during the mid-19th century.

2 RESIDENCE, WILLIAM McCOY, 410 S. FARMER STREET, 1856, ARCHITECT UNKNOWN. The first mayor of Independence, William McCoy, built this two-story antebellum home after the birth of two children in his family. Situated on a hill in front of the Truman Library, this residence has porches with bracketed Italianate posts and Ionic columns, bracketed eaves, white trim and a pitched roof. It is said that the structure's root cellar was a hiding place for persons wanted by Civil War soldiers.

**3** MARSHAL'S HOUSE AND COUNTY JAIL MUSEUM, 217 N. MAIN STREET, 1859, ARCHITECT UNKNOWN. Restored by the Jackson County Historical Society, this historic Federal-style building houses the society's headquarters. The structure also contains a museum that features renovated rooms decorated in 19th century style, including three bedrooms, a parlor, six jail cells and a collection of Civil War artifacts. Frank James, brother and cohort of Jesse James, awaited trial here after he surrendered.

**4** VAILE MANSION, 1500 N. LIBERTY STREET, 1881, ASA BEEBE CROSS. Designed by a pre-eminent Kansas City architect, this Second Empire style residence was built for Harvey Merrick Vaile. The mansion was put to many uses — originally a residence, it became successively a hotel, a sanitarium, and a nursing home. In 1974, the exterior was restored by Waldmar Kurok. Its style is conveyed by its Mansard roof, towered massing and ornate window, eave and roof trim.

Independence, Missouri

**5** TRUMAN HOME, 219 N. DELAWARE STREET, 1867, JAMES M. ADAMS; ADDITION, 1885, ARCHITECT UNKNOWN. This Victorian-style residence was the home of President and Mrs. Harry S. Truman from the time of their marriage in 1919. Originally, the house belonged to Mrs. Truman's father, a prominent Independence businessman. During Truman's presidency, the house served as the "summer White House."

**6** FLOURNEY HOUSE, 1233 W. LEXINGTON AVENUE, c.1826, ARCHITECT UNKNOWN. One of the town's oldest residences, this structure was built for Jones H. Flourney, a merchant and trader. Independence residents have fought for its survival and in order to save it from demolition, it was moved several times. It has now been restored and returned to its original site.

**7** REORGANIZED CHURCH OF JESUS CHRIST OF LATTER-DAY SAINTS TEMPLE, CORNER OF RIVER ROAD AND WALNUT STREET, 1992, HELLMUTH, OBATA & KASSABAUM, INC. In the early 19th century, Joseph Smith, founder of the Mormon Church, announced his belief that Independence was the location where Jesus would appear for his "Second Coming." Since that time Mormons have congregated in the area and established the Reorganized Church of Jesus Christ of Latter-day Saints headquarters here. Formally dedicated in 1994, this temple houses a 1,600-seat sanctuary and a Casavant pipe organ with 5,685 pipes and also features a breathtaking 300-foot roof that resembles a seashell. Limestone blocks and glass windows clad the exterior and stainless steel sheathing wraps around the temple spire.

WORLD HEADQUARTERS RLDS AUDITORIUM, 1001 W. WALNUT, 1926, HENRY C. SMITH, BLOOMGARTEN AND FROHWERK, AND JOSEPH MARTIN. A 211-foot, free-span dome covers the 6,000-seat assembly hall, which is used for church activities as well as civic and cultural functions. The auditorium houses a 6,189-pipe Aeolian-Skinner Company organ — one of the world's largest.

**8** RESIDENCE, OVERFELT-JOHNSON, 305 S. PLEASANT, c.1850, ARCHITECT UNKNOWN. Built for a successful mill owner, this Carpenter Gothic residence retains its original mid-19th century appearance including a steep gable roof, wall dormers, and jigsaw porch and eave elements.

**9** TRUMAN COURTHOUSE, 112 W. LEXINGTON, 1933, KEENE AND SIMPSON, AND DAVID FREDERICK. In 1932, Judge Harry S. Truman directed the renovation and remodeling of the Independence Courthouse, which would incorporate portions of six earlier Jackson County Courthouses. In 1948, Truman announced his intention to run for the presidency from this building. The design of the building was inspired by Independence Hall in Philadelphia. The Jackson County Parks and Recreation Department has restored Truman's office and courtroom, now open to the public.

**10** SERMON RESIDENCE, 701 PROCTOR PLACE, 1935, ARCHITECT UNKNOWN. This extravagant limestone, wood and shingled home reflects the high quality of residences in the Englewood neighborhood near Winner Road. The asymmetrical towered form, steeply pitched roof and masonry cladding convey the building's French Revival style.

**11** ROBERT T. SERMON COMMUNITY CENTER, 201 N. DODGION STREET, 1902, ARCHITECT UNKNOWN; RENOVATION, 1978, SHAUGHNESSY FICKEL & SCOTT ARCHITECTS. In 1902, the Dodgion Street Power Plant was built and provided power to Independence for more than 50 years. Relieved of its original function, the building stood empty until community members voiced the desire to redevelop the structure as a community center. Much of the original masonry façade and many of the Palladian windows were refurbished, and horizontal metal panels were added to accent the new complex.

**12** NATIONAL FRONTIER TRAILS CENTER, 318 W. PACIFIC STREET, 1990, SHAUGHNESSY FICKEL & SCOTT ARCHITECTS. This 20,100 square-foot multipurpose visitors' center commemorates those who traveled through Independence on their way to the Western frontier. The entry courtyard features a freestanding colonnade that defines the edge of the an area and provides space for group activity.

**13** GRACELAND COLLEGE, 1401 W. TRUMAN ROAD, 1998, CDFM² ARCHITECTURE AND MACKEY MITCHELL ZAHNER. Located in the Midtown Truman Road Corridor, this 55,000 square-foot building was constructed as an extension of Graceland College, based in Lamoni, Iowa. The brick structure houses the School of Nursing and includes technologically advanced classroom spaces, a health promotions center, skills labs and a 250-seat auditorium.

14 SHEET METAL WORKERS LOCAL NO. 2 UNION HALL AND OFFICE, 2902 BLUE RIDGE BOULEVARD, 1989, SHAUGHNESSY FICKEL & SCOTT ARCHITECTS. This union hall and office appropriately utilize sheet metal to create a functional and decorative structure. The use of industrial materials spotlights the craftsmanship of the builders and sheet metal workers.

15 UNITED MISSOURI BANK, 16900 GUDGELL ROAD, 1996, GOULD EVANS GOODMAN ASSOCIATES. The main section of the brick bank is a square box that supports a tower that resembles a lighthouse.

Independence, Missouri

# Kansas City, Kansas

REFLECTING SOME OF THE METROPOLITAN REGION'S richest cultural diversity, Kansas City, Kansas, lies west of the confluence of the Kansas and Missouri Rivers.

Part of the Delaware Indian Reservation created in 1818, some of this land was sold to the Wyandot Indians in 1843 and developed into a trading post called Wyandot City which contained the first free school in Kansas, a church, a community store and a council house. White settlers began moving to the area, and in 1859 wrote the constitution under which Kansas gained statehood. Kansas City was formed in 1886 with the merger of four residential communities: Armourdale, Armstrong, Wyandotte and a piece of land across the Kaw River. Later, the settlements of Argentine and Rosedale were annexed.

In the 1890s, European immigrants began flocking to Kansas City because of its proximity to factories and job opportunities near the rivers. Croatian, Polish, Russian, German and Slovenian families worked in nearby packing plants, rail yards, grain elevators and refineries.

Kansas City, Kansas, remains a regional industrial center and ethnically diverse community, and its architecture reflects these influences. Historic neighborhoods, such as Strawberry Hill and the Westheight Manor Historic District, distinguish this area of the metroplex.

207

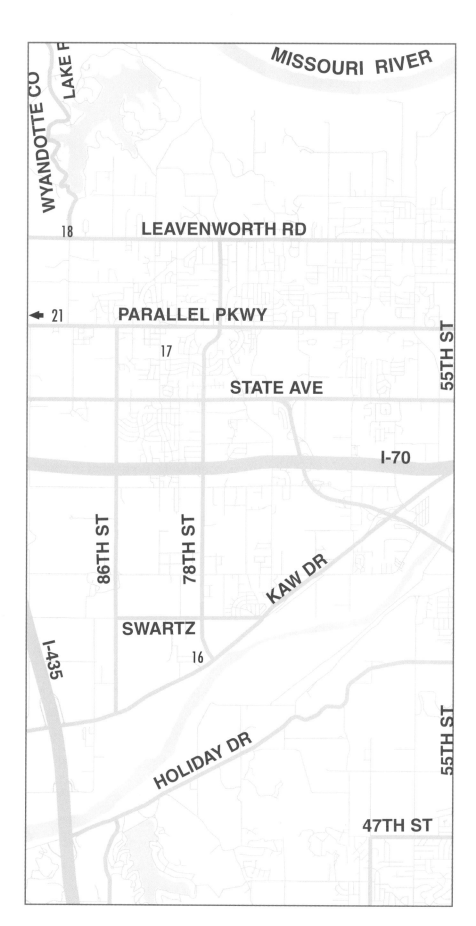

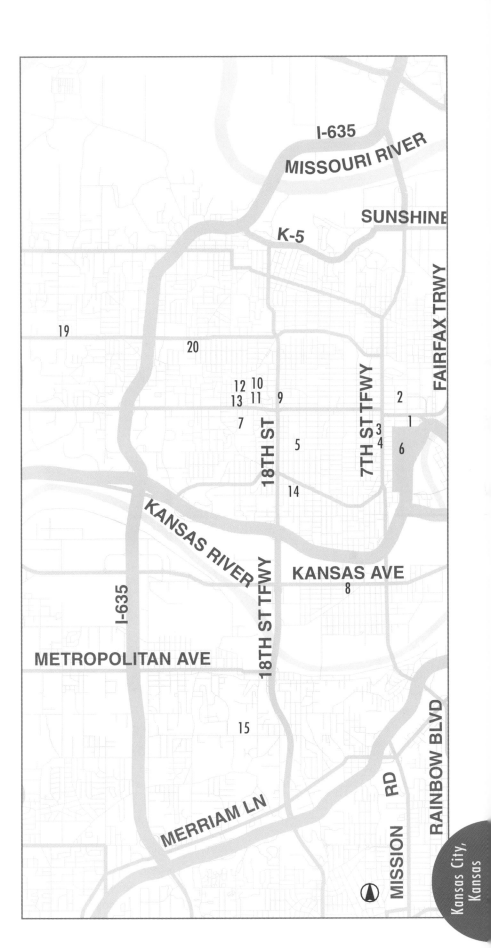

I-635

MISSOURI RIVER

SUNSHINE

K-5

FAIRFAX TRWY

19

20

7TH ST FWY

12 10
13 11 9

2

18TH ST

7

3
1

5

4
6

14

KANSAS RIVER

18TH ST FWY

KANSAS AVE

8

I-635

METROPOLITAN AVE

18TH ST FWY

RAINBOW BLVD

15

MERRIAM LN

MISSION RD

Kansas City,
Kansas

1 ENVIRONMENTAL PROTECTION AGENCY REGION 7 OFFICE, 901 N. FIFTH STREET, 1999, LANGDON WILSON. The EPA commissioned this five-story, 200,000 square-foot building to promote environmentally and economically sound construction practices. Its brick exterior features geometric, recessed windows, exterior light shelves to enhance natural lighting, and "green" building materials. The interior has a large glass- and steel-covered atrium filled with trees and a fountain that enhance air and sound quality. Outdoor terraces complete the overall environment.

2 U.S. POSTAL SERVICE CIVIC CENTER STATION, 550 NEBRASKA AVENUE, 1987, EUGENE BUCHANAN. This 11,687 square-foot federal building has dark glass windows with steel frames and beige masonry units and horizontal banding.

**3** WYANDOTTE COUNTY COURTHOUSE, 710 N. SEVENTH STREET, 1927, WIGHT AND WIGHT. The Wight brothers, who designed many impressive government structures in the Kansas City area during the early 20th century, received the commission to design this beaux-arts building after winning an architectural competition. The focus of the limestone structure is a massive colonnade at the entrance.

**4** SOLDIERS AND SAILORS MEMORIAL BUILDING (MEMORIAL HALL), 600 N. SEVENTH STREET TRAFFICWAY, 1925, ROSE AND PETERSON; AUDITORIUM, 1937, JOSEPH RADOTINSKY. In 1921, a bond issue supported the construction of this building as a memorial to the 6,500 men from Wyandotte County who served in World War I. The structure's exterior features a Classical portico supported by six Tuscan stone columns. Brown brick clads the walls, and stone and terra cotta ornamentation adorn the façade. The elaborate interior holds meeting rooms, office space and a large auditorium. For a short time soon after the construction of the building, the Veterans of Foreign Wars Association was housed here. The building's 3,300-seat auditorium hosts sporting, cultural, religious and entertainment events.

**5** ST. PETER'S CATHOLIC CHURCH (CATHEDRAL OF ST. PETER), 414 N. GRANDVIEW BOULEVARD, 1927, HENRY W. BRINKMAN. This French Gothic church, the seat of the Archdiocese of Kansas City, is distinguished by a 145-foot bell tower and some of the area's finest stained glass windows, which were installed in 1942. The façade is split-faced granite, and the main altar and other interior appointments are made of Carrara marble imported from Italy.

**6** STRAWBERRY HILL NEIGHBORHOOD, FOURTH STREET AREA. One of the area's oldest and best-known ethnic neighborhoods, Strawberry Hill is rich in cultural history. In the early 1900s, Eastern European immigrants, who worked in nearby meat-packing houses for as little as 10 cents an hour, began occupying houses on the eastern slope of "Splitlog's Hill." Mathias Splitlog was a Native American who owned and developed the hill that overlooks the Missouri and Kansas rivers and the West Bottoms. Croatian and Slovenian immigrants occupied rows of two-, three- and four-room homes that sold for around $500 and rented for $1 a month. The Strawberry Hill Museum and Cultural Center, located at 720 N. Fourth Street in a Queen Anne-style structure, preserves the area's Eastern European customs and culture.

**7** WYANDOTTE HIGH SCHOOL, 2501 MINNESOTA AVENUE, 1937, HAMILTON, FELLOWS AND NEDVED ARCHITECTS, AND JOSEPH RADOTINSKY. When a fire destroyed the previous high school, this building was built during the Depression with WPA funds. Fronted by two huge towers with arched openings and multicolored brickwork, the complex was designed in a figure eight pattern with two pentagon buildings connected by a gymnasium and a cafeteria. Sculptor Emil Zettler employed stylized floral patterns and pre-Columbian Indian decorations on the exterior buttresses and the arches, and Romanesque ornament on the column capitals.

**8** RESIDENCE, ANTHONY SAUER (SAUER CASTLE), 945 SHAWNEE ROAD, 1872, ARCHITECT UNKNOWN. Built for a German immigrant, businessman and area leader, this structure is one of the earliest and finest Italianate villas in the state. The three-story, 12-room house is remarkable for its main feature, a four-story, square tower. Most of the building's materials, including the exterior red brick and the elegant wood used in the interior, were shipped from St. Louis, and the furnishings were ordered from Europe. Reportedly haunted, the Sauer Castle has been a popular Halloween destination for years.

Kansas City, Kansas

**9** WESTHEIGHT MANOR HISTORIC DISTRICT, NORTH 18TH STREET TO NORTH 25TH STREET, STATE AVENUE TO WOOD AVENUE, 1915-1916, HARE & HARE, PLANNERS AND LANDSCAPE ARCHITECTS. Originally the estate of Hanford Kerr, the land was subdivided and developed into an exclusive neighborhood by Jesse Hoel with the backing of J.O. Fife and Hanford Kerr. Distinguished by the planning of Hare & Hare, designers of many Kansas City, Missouri, parks and boulevards, the subdivision boasts homes designed by the area's finest architects, including Louis S. Curtiss and Edward Buehler Delk.

**10** RESIDENCE, JESSE A. HOEL, 2108 WASHINGTON BOULEVARD, 1916, LOUIS S. CURTISS. Jesse Hoel, a real estate magnate and the catalyst behind the development of the Westheight Manor neighborhood, commissioned this Prairie School-style residence built in the middle of the district. Stonework and overhanging eaves emphasize its low, horizontal lines. The use of exterior tile, trellises, planting boxes and detailing on the woodwork lend an Oriental flair to the residence.

**11** RESIDENCE, HARRY G. MILLER SR., 2204 WASHINGTON BOULEVARD, 1921, LOUIS S. CURTISS. When Harry Miller, owner of the Kansas City Pattern and Model Works, decided to build his home in Westheight Manor, he hired Louis S. Curtiss, who wanted to create "The House of the Future." Similar to the Tromanhauser residence (3603 W. Roanoke Drive, Kansas City, Missouri), the exterior of this house features stucco walls, trellis-patterned ornamentation, tile roof, and lighted clerestory panels in typical Curtiss style. This one-story, modern structure is said to be Curtiss' last design.

**12** RESIDENCE, THOMAS M. TORSON, 2300 WASHINGTON BOULEVARD, 1923, VICTOR J. DEFOE. Located on the highest ground in Westheight, this $40,000 residence reflects the Progressive movement and the American Arts and Crafts bungalow style. The low, red-tiled, hipped roof and bands of casement windows enhance the strong, horizontal lines of the grey limestone structure.

**13** Fire Station No. 9, 2 S. 14th Street, 1911, William E. Harris; renovation, 1979, Solomon Claybaugh and Young. A mixture of motifs, this structure imitates the neighborhood's eclectic combination of architecture with elements of Classic Revival, Tudor Revival and Prairie styles. Playful firemen gargoyles, complete with hoses, adorn the corners of the building.

**14** Westminster Court, North 24th Street and Nebraska Avenue, 1924, Courtland Van Brunt and Edward Buehler Delk. Hoel Realty Company developed this residential court to imitate the English "garden city" concept. Five houses and two duplexes, all two-story, wood frame and stucco structures, surround a landscaped court area that leads to the entrance of the development.

**15** J.C. Harmon High School, 2400 Steele Road, 1974, Marshall and Brown. Similar to their work on the Penn Valley Community College and Johnson County Community College, Marshall and Brown designed this education center as an L-shaped, two-story structure, placing the gymnasium and cafeteria in the center of the complex. Its brown blocks and steel-framed windows give the structure an industrial look.

**16** Residence, Moses Grinter (Grinter Place), 1420 S. 78th Street, 1857, John Swagger. Moses Grinter, reportedly the first white settler in Wyandotte County, built this Greek Revival house. Grinter operated the first commercial ferry to cross the Kansas River in 1831. The structure's brick was made on-site of mud and animal hair, and its walnut and white pine lumber arrived by oxcart from Leavenworth, Kansas. The Kansas State Historical Society maintains the house as a museum.

**17** WEST WYANDOTTE BRANCH LIBRARY, 1737 N. 82ND STREET, 1986, EUGENE BUCHANAN. The various shapes and textures of this building lend a feeling of discontinuity that was designed to create excitement. The exterior includes rounded brick and terraced walls, arched windows and various open spaces.

**18** JAMES P. DAVIS HALL, 91ST STREET AND LEAVENWORTH ROAD, 1937, ARCHITECT UNKNOWN. Constructed during the Depression as part of the WPA project to build the Wyandotte County Lake Park, this rustic lodge structure was built from native limestone and hand-hewn oak beams. Most of the building's materials were found on-site.

**19** TRINITY UNITED METHODIST CHURCH, 5010 PARALLEL PARKWAY, 1965, A. HENSEL FINK. This modern, stone church features large stained-glass windows that depict Christian themes and stories. A 38-foot window dominates the main elevation.

**20** SEVENTH-DAY ADVENTIST CHURCH CENTRAL STATES CONFERENCE CENTER (MATHER HALL, ST. AUGUSTINE HALL), 3301 PARALLEL PARKWAY, 1896, VRYDAGH AND WOLFE; CHAPEL ADDITION, 1938, H.T. LIEBERT AND JOSEPH RADOTINSKY. Samuel F. Mather bequeathed this land to the Methodist Protestant Church to build a coeducational university. This Richardsonian Romanesque stone structure cost $40,000 and was the centerpiece of Kansas City University, which began in 1896 with six professors and 50 students. The Augustinian Recollects, a Catholic monastic order, purchased the property after the university closed due to financial difficulties. The order added a modern chapel at the rear of the hall. The building now serves as a regional conference headquarters for the Seventh-day Adventist Church.

**21** MAYWOOD COMMUNITY CHURCH, 11201 PARALLEL PARKWAY, 1883, ARCHITECT UNKNOWN; RENOVATION AND ADDITION, 1938, RAY BYERS. Originally the Cumberland Presbyterian Church, organized in 1869, this simple, wood-frame structure exhibits a tall, peaked tower and is one of best examples in the area of a vernacular-style church.

# People's Choice Awards

KANSAS CITIANS TAKE GREAT PRIDE IN ARCHITECTURAL AND PUBLIC ART achievements that distinguish the five-county region. To celebrate the public's enthusiasm, *Star Magazine* of *The Kansas City Star* and the AIA/KC asked Kansas Citians to vote on their favorite area landmarks and public art.

The published survey offered the public more than 40 choices of structures and public art pieces featured in this guide, including:

## LANDMARKS

New York Life Building • Municipal Auditorium • Union Station • Liberty Memorial • Giralda Tower • Country Club Plaza • Harry S. Truman Sports Complex • St. Francis Xavier Catholic Church • RLDS Temple • Powell Gardens Chapel & Visitors Center • Kansas City Museum • Midland Theater • Standard/Folly Theater • Kansas City Power & Light Co. Building • Nelson-Atkins Museum of Art • Bartle Hall • Kansas City International Airport • Deramus Education Pavilion at the Kansas City Zoo • 7500 W. 110th Street • Charles Evans Whittaker U.S. Courthouse • Bernard Corrigan Residence • United Missouri Bank Headquarters • The Walnuts Apartments • Grace and Holy Trinity Cathedral • Boley Clothing Company Building • Temple B'nai Jehudah • Truman Library • Truman Home • Westheight Neighborhood

## PUBLIC ART

*Shuttlecocks*, Claes Oldenburg and Coosje van Bruggen, Nelson-Atkins Museum • *Sky Stations*, R.M. Fischer, Bartle Hall • J.C. Nichols Memorial Fountain, Henri Greber, 47th and Main Streets • *Spirit of Freedom* Fountain, Richard Hunt, Cleveland Street and Brush Creek • *The Scout*, Cyrus Dallin, Penn Valley Park • *The Bronze Boar*, Benelli, 47th Street and Wornall Road • *Walking Man (On The Edge)*, Jonathan Borofsky, Johnson County Community College/Oppenheimer-Stein Sculpture Collection • *Triple Crown*, Kenneth Snelson, Crown Center • *Bird Lives*, Robert Graham, 18th and Vine Streets • *Spider, 1997*, Louise Bourgeois, Kemper Museum of Art

The public responded with more than 6,500 votes during a two-month period. Voters also added write-in selections, especially for Cathedral of the Immaculate Conception, St. Mary's Episcopal Church, *Children's Fountain*, *Growing* at Leawood City Hall, and *Pioneer Mother*.

Top choices for landmarks, in order, were Liberty Memorial, Union Station and the Nelson-Atkins Museum of Art. For public art, voters chose the J.C. Nichols Memorial Fountain, *The Scout* at Penn Valley Park and *Shuttlecocks*.

# ontributors

AIA GUIDEBOOK STEERING AND EDITORIAL COMMITTEE
Bryan Gross, AIA, guidebook committee chairman
Tom Bean, AIA, president, AIA/KC 2000
Charles Cassias, AIA, president, AIA/KC 1999
Richard Farnan, AIA
Wayne Feuerborn
Cary Goodman, FAIA
Susan Richards Johnson, AIA
Elizabeth Rosin
Blair Sands, public art administrator, Municipal Art Commission
Michael Shaughnessy, AIA
Greg Sheldon, AIA
Joy Swallow, AIA
Anita Valdavia, executive director, AIA/KC


THIS BOOK WAS CREATED BY HIGHWATER EDITIONS, A DIVISION OF JANE MOBLEY ASSOCIATES

RESEARCH
Stacey Million
Elizabeth Rosin

WRITING
Stacey Million
Jane Mobley
Elizabeth Rosin

EDITING
Jane Mobley
Tom Bean
Bryan Gross
Blair Sands
Stacey Million
Elizabeth Rosin
Linda Lakemacher
Sarah Woelfel
Rea Wilson
Hannah Lucas

DESIGN
Sära Keehn

PRINCIPAL PHOTOGRAPHY
Brad Finch

·

ADDITIONAL PHOTOGRAPHY CONTRIBUTED BY:
Architectural Fotographics
ASAI Architects
David Bean
BNIM Architects
By Design/Kansas City, P.C.
CDFM² Architecture
Cleveland Chiropractic College Archives
Ellerbe Becket
Gastinger Walker Harden Architects, Inc.
Gould Evans Goodman Associates
David Greusel, AIA
HNTB Corporation
Charles Howard, AIA
Roy Inman (Marjorie Powell Allen Chapel at Powell Gardens)
International Architects Atelier
Bruce Mathews (Aviation Department Administration Building)
Mathews Communications
Eric Morehouse, Assoc. AIA
Peckham Guyton Albers & Viets, Inc.
Clayton Porsch, AIA
Powell Gardens, Inc.
Rafael Architects, Inc.
Shaughnessy Fickel & Scott Architects
Shaw Hofstra + Associates
WRS Architects, Inc.
TK Architects


ADDITIONAL HISTORICAL DATA PROVIDED BY:
Hallmark Cards, Inc.
Historic Preservation Services
Independence Historical Society
Johnson County Chamber of Commerce
Kansas City Art Institute and Library
Kansas State Historical Society
Kemper Museum of Contemporary Art
Landmarks Commission, City of Kansas City, Missouri
Landmarks Commission, City of Kansas City, Kansas
Missouri Valley Room, Kansas City Public Library
Municipal Art Commission
Museums at 18th and Vine
Parks and Recreation, City of Kansas City, Missouri
Powell Gardens, Inc.
Special Collections, Kansas City Public Library
Union Station

Contributors

# Suggested Further Reading

Bradley, Lenore K., *CORINTHIAN HALL: AN AMERICAN PALACE ON GLADSTONE*. Kansas City, Mo.: Lowell Press, 1981.

Brown, A. Theodore and Lyle W. Dorsett, *K.C.: A HISTORY OF KANSAS CITY, MISSOURI*. Boulder, Colo.: Pruett Publishing Co., 1978.

Case, Theodore S., *HISTORY OF KANSAS CITY, MISSOURI*. Syracuse, N.Y.: D. Mason & Co., 1888.

Comee, Fred T., "LOUIS CURTISS OF KANSAS CITY". *Progressive Architecture*. August, 1963: 128-34 (reprint).

DeAngelo, Dory, *KANSAS CITY STYLE: A SOCIAL AND CULTURAL HISTORY OF KANSAS CITY AS SEEN THROUGH ITS LOST ARCHITECTURE*. Kansas City, Mo.: Fifield Publishing Co., 1992.

DeAngelo, Dory, *WHAT ABOUT KANSAS CITY! A HISTORICAL HANDBOOK*. Kansas City, Mo.: Two Lane Press, 1997.

Ehrlich, George, *KANSAS CITY, MISSOURI: AN ARCHITECTURAL HISTORY, 1826-1990*. Columbia, Mo.: University of Missouri Press, 1992.

Foerster, Bernd, *INDEPENDENCE, MISSOURI*. Independence, Mo.: The Heritage Commission, 1978.

Grant, W.D., *THE ROMANTIC PAST OF THE KANSAS CITY REGION, 1540-1880*. Kansas City, Mo.: Business Men's Assurance, 1987.

Hancks, Larry K., *A GIFT TO THE FUTURE: KANSAS CITY, KANSAS ARCHITECTURE*. Kansas City, Kan.: Board of Education, 1988.

Hancks, Larry K. and Meredith Roberts, *ROOTS: THE HISTORIC AND ARCHITECTURAL HERITAGE OF KANSAS CITY, KANSAS*. Kansas City, Kan.: Community Development Program, 1976.

Haskell, Henry C. Jr., and Richard B. Fowler, *CITY OF THE FUTURE: A NARRATIVE HISTORY OF KANSAS CITY, 1850-1950*. Kansas City, Mo.: Frank Glenn Publishing Co., Inc., 1950.

*HISTORIC KANSAS CITY ARCHITECTURE*. Kansas City, Mo.: Landmarks Commission of Kansas City, Missouri, 1975.

Historic Kansas City Foundation, *KANSAS CITY, MISSOURI: A DOWNTOWN TOUR*. Kansas City, Mo., 1984.

Hoffhaus, Charles E., *CHEZ LES CANSES, THREE CENTURIES AT KAWSMOUTH*. Kansas City, Mo.: The Lowell Press, 1984.

Hudson, David S., ed. *Focus Kansas City: A 24-Hour Heartland Portrait*. Prairie Village, Kan.: Harrow Books, 1989.

Majors, Alexander, *Seventy Years on the Frontier*. Chicago and New York: Rand McNally & Co., 1893.

Mitchell, Giles Carroll, *There is No Limit: Architecture and Sculpture in Kansas City*. Kansas City, Mo.: Brown-White Co., 1934.

Mobley, Jane and Nancy Whitnell Harris, *A City Within a Park: One Hundred Years of Parks and Boulevards in Kansas City, Missouri*. Kansas City, Mo.: American Society of Landscape Architects and the Kansas City, Missouri, Board of Parks & Recreation Commissioners, 1991.

Mobley, Jane and Shifra Stein, *Heart of America: Kansas City*. Montgomery, Ala.: Community Communications, 1994.

Montgomery, Rick and Shirl Kasper, *Kansas City: an American Story*. Kansas City, Mo.: Kansas City Star Books, 1999.

Perry, Milton F., et al. *Mulkey Square, Kansas City, Missouri, 1869-1973: A Survey of the City's First Suburb*. Kansas City, Mo.: Museums Council of Mid-America, 1973.

Sachs, David and George Ehrlich, *Guide to Kansas Architecture*. Lawrence, Kan.: University Press of Kansas, 1996.

Sandy, Wilda, *Here Lies Kansas City*. Kansas City, Mo.: Bennett Schneider, 1984.

Schirmer, Sherry Lamb and Richard D. McKinzie, *At the River's Bend: An Illustrated History of Kansas City, Independence and Jackson County*. Jackson County Historical Society. Woodland Hills, Calif.: Windsor Publications Inc., 1982.

Scott, Deborah Emont and Martin Friedman, *Modern Sculpture at the Nelson-Atkins Museum of Art: An Anniversary Celebration*. Kansas City, Mo.: The Nelson Gallery Foundation, 1999.

Simmons, Marc, *Along the Santa Fe Trail*. Albuquerque, N.M.: University of New Mexico Press, 1986.

Whitney, Carrie Westlake, *Kansas City, Missouri: Its History and its People*. Chicago: The S.J. Clarke Publishing Co., 1908.

Suggested Further Reading

# **I**ndex: Architecture & Public Art

# ⬤ndex: Architects & Artists

# W

# Y

Index:
Architects
& Artists

*AMERICAN INSTITUTE OF ARCHITECTS GUIDE TO KANSAS CITY ARCHITECTURE & PUBLIC ART*
WAS DIGITALLY COMPOSED IN
QUARKXPRESS USING THE
FUTURA FONT FAMILY AND PRINTED ON
CONSOLIDATED PAPER
FROSTBRITE MATTE TEXT AND
INTERNATIONAL PAPER
CAROLINA COATED-ONE-SIDE COVER